ACTIVE VOICE The Collection

The Real Life Adventures Of An Asian-American, Lesbian, Feminist, Activist And Her Friends!

ILLUSTRATION BY DAN PARENT

Anecdotes written by P. Kristen Enos
with Heidi Ho

Art by
Derek Chua, Leesamarie Croal, Casandra Grullon, Beth Varni
with Dan Parent

PUBLISHED BY FURIA PRESS.
ALL RIGHTS RESERVED.

ISBN: 0986295930
ISBN 13: 978-0986295935

PRINTER: CREATESPACE INDEPENDENT PUBLISHING PLATFORM, NORTH CHARLESTON, SC

ACTIVE VOICE The Comic Collection

Table Of Contents

FORWARD

By Joseph Amster

This collection of stories originated as a column in the Orange County and Long Beach Blade Newsmagazine. Kristen Enos was involved with the magazine from its inception in 1992, appearing on the publication's first cover. Most of the columns were written during my stint as editor from 1996-2003. Her first-person columns were always a good read, usually mixing stories from her life around contemporary issues. Entertaining, often irreverent, they serve as a document of a specific time and place: Orange County, California in the late 1980s to 1990s.

Many will, no doubt, find it hard to believe that there was LGBT life in Orange County during this period. After all, this was home to a triumvirate of some of America's worst homophobes: Congressmembers Bob Dornan, William Dannemeyer, and the Traditional Values Coalition's Lou Sheldon. Homophobia was rampant, conferences like The Preservation of the Heterosexual Ethic were staged, opposition to Orange County's first LGBT Pride Parade and Festival was fierce, the City of Irvine rescinded their human rights ordinance, and AIDS cut a swath of death across Laguna Beach and other cities. Yet, within this atmosphere of oppression, a thriving LGBT community existed and grew. Activist organizations like the Orange County Visibility League, ACTUP, Queer Nation, and numerous political and social groups were established in this period, as well as the University of California Irvine's LGBT Resource Center. It was there that Kristen, during her college days, became an activist. It is also out of this crucible that the Orange County and Long Beach Blade grew.

Kristen's column was always a joy to read, and I looked forward to its monthly appearance in my inbox (always before deadline). Her unique perspective intrigued and informed me, as it did many of the magazine's readers.

Today we are all older, the Blade seems to have ceased publication (as did many LGBT newspapers and magazines nationwide), and while homophobia still exists, it is not nearly as blatant or acceptable as it was in the '80s and '90s. Kristen's columns serve as an important document of those times, seen through her eyes, and I am overjoyed that they have found a new life and audience through this delightful graphic novel.

Welcome

By P. Kristen Enos

This book was over thirty years in the making, with many versions and starts and stops. From my "adventures," both in the queer community and my own personal life, I wanted such stories to be documented and made public as reality is sometimes far more interesting than fiction. I certainly hope you enjoy this collection because there are definitely more that can be written and drawn.

And as the book subtitle states, these adventures wouldn't have happened without my friends (and coworkers.)

So in the spirit of giving credit and thanks as needed, the following people were instrumental in putting this particular book together:

Nicolas (Nico) Martinez Jr.
Joseph Amster (and Rick Shelton)
Julie Tanit (and Lisa Kaye and Rachel Pena)
Heidi Ho and her mother, brother and cousin
My fabulous team of story artists (in alphabetical order by last name):
      Derek, Leesamarie, Casandra and Beth
John Duran
Laura Poor
Kirsten Dernbach
Dan Parent

A special thanks of support to Jill Marr

And finally: David Etheridge for giving me the opportunity to create the original "Active Voice" column, and Bill LaPointe and Rus Calisch for continuing to support it in The Blade.

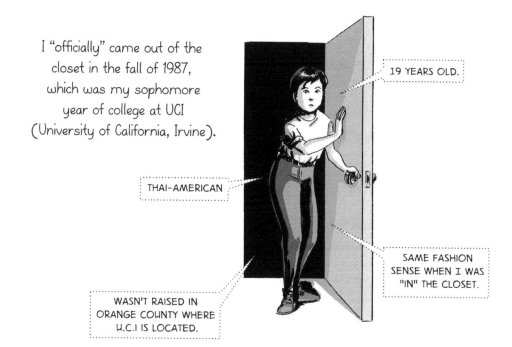

I "officially" came out of the closet in the fall of 1987, which was my sophomore year of college at UCI (University of California, Irvine).

19 YEARS OLD.

THAI-AMERICAN

SAME FASHION SENSE WHEN I WAS "IN" THE CLOSET.

WASN'T RAISED IN ORANGE COUNTY WHERE U.C.I IS LOCATED.

While I had a lot of great friends from having lived in the dorms the previous year, I didn't know anyone who was gay or lesbian.

At least not that I knew of. Being out wasn't the "thing" back then.

Since this was before the Internet, finding ways to meet other people like me was a challenge.

I first tried the UCI phone book to see what was on campus.

I spotted an entry for the Gay & Lesbian Student Union with a campus address.

But the office was always closed no matter what time or day I stopped by.

And there wasn't information about meetings or events on the office door or answering machine recording.

But when I'm faced with a challenge, I become more determined.

I can't remember exactly how but I found out that AIDS Walk Orange County was looking for volunteers.

But as a poor college student without a car, it meant a looong bus ride to Newport Beach.

BACKPACK OF TEXTBOOKS

Without a Thomas Guide, G.P.S. or Siri, I had to find the address based on answering machine directions.

I eventually found the AIDS Walk OC HQ in a tiny office building.

I had no idea what to expect of this experience as I stood in the parking lot.

There were only a couple of people there, but they were immediately welcoming.

I never said "Hey, I'm a lesbian" but that wasn't necessary at all.

And I was just sooo glad to be there!

They quickly introduced me to the standard volunteer tasks of the late 80's.

Envelope stuffing for bulk mailings

Data entry

Cold calling

And I discovered the all too important volunteer "payment" of free pizza and soda

I was only there for a few hours but I felt extreme satisfaction of time well spent for a great cause.

As a starving college student, I admit this was crucial, too.

When I left, I was completely on cloud nine.

NOT EVEN NOTICING THE WEIGHT OF THE TEXTBOOKS THAT I ENDED UP NOT USING

I was barely aware of my surroundings as I crossed a one-way street back to the bus stop.

- HONK! -

Hey, I remember Vietnam!

I was completely caught off guard as a flurry of thoughts went through my mind.

I'm NOT Vietnamese!

You weren't even *born* back then!

My Dad was a Vietnam vet!

You're NOT calling me a "dyke"?!

But they clearly didn't count on me having the background of being a mouthy, rebellious teenager (according to my parents).

Their reaction of joking laughter revealed how they thought that harassing me was just a FUN thing to do.

I fantasized about what I wish I had done instead.

But it RUINED my mood!

What good will I had moments before was COMPLETELY gone!

COLLEGE TEXTBOOKS, REMEMBER?

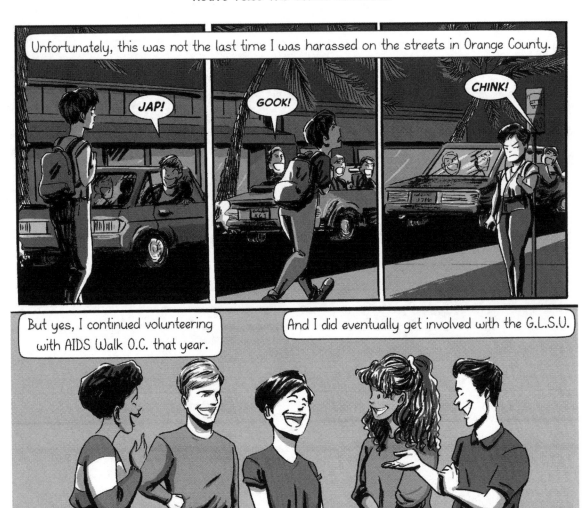

But that first harassment incident showed that the fighter in me came out when needed.

A trait needed to be an activist.

Of course, it was only the beginning of what was an unplanned calling.

Though I admit if they had actually called me "dyke," I probably would've attacked them.

– END –

The Most Interesting Thing

Story: P. Kristen Enos — Art: Leesamarie Croal

On Aug. 31 1992, I was hired into my first real job.

The company was in Irvine, California, about an hour south of Los Angeles.

I was 24 at the time and my prior work experience consisted of temp assignments and part-time college student stints.

I was already familiar with the work environment and people because I had been a temp at this company for a couple of years.

At the time, I had no desire for any long term career in the corporate world.

Gay and Lesbian Pride

I viewed it as a necessary evil to pay my bills and allow me to do whatever I wanted in my personal time.

Even as a temp, I was never "closeted" at work but I am a respecter of "appropriate time and place." Those coworkers who became friends I told, and others I didn't.

And I was perfectly fine with the idea of having the rumor mill do the coming out for me.

I'M A LESBIAN.

PSST!

PSST!

PSST!

Because there wasn't a large enough conference room in our office building to hold all employees, we would have our quarterly meetings at a nearby hotel. This is where we would be brought up to speed on the latest company news and upcoming activities.

I never attended one of these meetings before, so I was excited to go as an official employee.

One of the standard agenda items for this meeting is that all employees who had been hired in the previous quarter would stand and quickly introduce themselves. I wasn't into cheesy things like that but I was encouraged to play along.

This time, the meeting facilitator thought it would be fun for people to introduce themselves with: your name, the date you were hired, the department you worked in...

... and the MOST INTERESTING THING about yourself.

The first thought that went through my mind was "Wait, I'm supposed to tell them I'm a LESBIAN?!"

I know I didn't HAVE to, but that's what immediately went through my mind.

The year before, in 1991, California Governor Pete Wilson had vetoed AB 101, a law to include sexual orientation as a protected class against discrimination in the workplace.

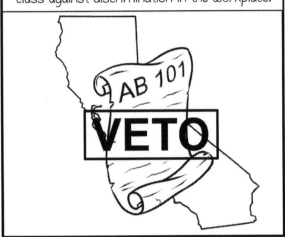

This naturally outraged all queer activists (and their friends and allies) into massive protest rallies throughout the state.

And while politics aren't my thing, (I considered myself a social activist), I am a supporter and a journalist.

To add more complexity to our situation, my friends and I lived and worked in Orange County, which was known as "The Orange Curtain" because of its reputation of being a bastion of conservatism in the state.

SAN FRANCISCO

LOS ANGELES

SAN DIEGO

Gov. Wilson finally signed the bill into law in September 1992, less than a month after I was hired.

The bill was now signed so I didn't feel as if there was a need to come out on a large scale to help the cause.

Work time was part of my private time and not subject to my activist standards.

But with the conversations of my lesbian activities with these work friends, I felt a certain...

EXPECTATION.

I decided to take my cue by how personal other people's revelations would be.

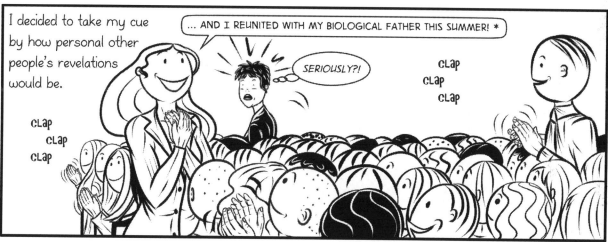

... AND I REUNITED WITH MY BIOLOGICAL FATHER THIS SUMMER! *

SERIOUSLY?!

CLaP CLaP CLaP

CLaP CLaP CLaP

*Yes, the woman really did say that.

That declaration triggered my innate demand for equal and fair treatment, even to the point of being obnoxious. Yet...

My turn:

HI, I'M KRISTEN ENOS. I WAS HIRED ON AUGUST 31ST AFTER BEING A TEMP FOR 2 YEARS. I AM IN THE BILLING DEPARTMENT...

... AND THE **SECOND** MOST INTERESTING THING ABOUT ME

IS THAT I'VE BEEN A **COMIC BOOK** READER SINCE I WAS 6 YEARS OLD.*

* Yes, I really said this. And I still think my being into comics was more controversial in some circles than my lesbianism.

Did I cop out? Maybe not according to EVERYONE.

HA HA HA

CO-WORKERS WHO "KNEW"

HA HA HA

And given comments that I overheard, some people were confused:

BUT WHAT'S HER **MOST** INTERESTING THING?

I DON'T KNOW.

I DON'T GET IT.

No one ever asked me my Most Interesting Thing even though I worked in that department for several years.

I just assumed that meant that anyone who really wanted to know, already KNEW, which meant I did my activist job, right?

– END –

When I came out in the Fall of '87 as a student at UC Irvine, I wasn't socially queer-connected.

To make friends, I wanted to participate in anything that didn't require a car, money or a penis.

So when the Co-Chairs of the GLSU announced a need for people to march in the upcoming Long Beach Pride Parade, I immediately volunteered.

We would march behind a banner that was a long piece of paper colored by markers and paint.

U.C. IRVINE GAY, & LESBIAN

That Sunday morning we were to meet at the admin building flag pole then carpool up to the Long Beach pride parade setup area.

But only a few of us showed up, and I was the only woman.

CO-CHAIR

WHERE *IS* EVERYONE?

It was the first time I became aware of how complex being "out and visible" could be.

I had never seen a gay pride parade before. Everything I knew were from obnoxious images of drag queens in mainstream newspapers meant to shock and appall their readers.

Those images probably inspired me to want to march in the parade because I knew my friends and I didn't look like that.

When we arrived at the parade setup area, I didn't know what to expect.

I saw for the first time examples of queer diversity that I had never seen before.

DYKES ON BIKES

A VARIETY OF DRAG QUEENS NOT SHOWN IN MAINSTREAM MEDIA

SUPPORT ORGANIZATIONS

POLITICAL GROUPS

That morning I couldn't help but notice the irony in my first real-life exposure to a pride parade was as a participant.

While I was disappointed that a lot of GLSU members had not shown up, I dismissed it as everyone being, well, *college students.*

I also didn't realize there were fears of exposure.

From the risk of being seen by someone who could report back to their parents.

Newspapers and television would cover the event.

So the fear of being recorded was at a terrifying level.

Since I wasn't from Southern California, it never occurred to me NOT to participate for those reasons.

Once the parade started, I was able to fully basked in the glory and, yes, PRIDE as we walk down the parade route with cheers from those who watched.

Until that one moment...

U.C.I., WHERE ARE YOUR WOMEN?!

SHE'S RIGHT HERE!

THEY WERE PARTYING TOO HARD LAST NIGHT!*

... where I was reminded that sometimes you just can't win *everything*.

* THIS IS NICO. WE DIDN'T KNOW IT AT THE TIME BUT WE WOULD DEVELOP A FRIENDSHIP THAT WOULD LAST 30 YEARS AND COUNTING.

– END –

That Orange County (Cultural) Pride

Story: P. Kristen Enos – Art: Derek Chua

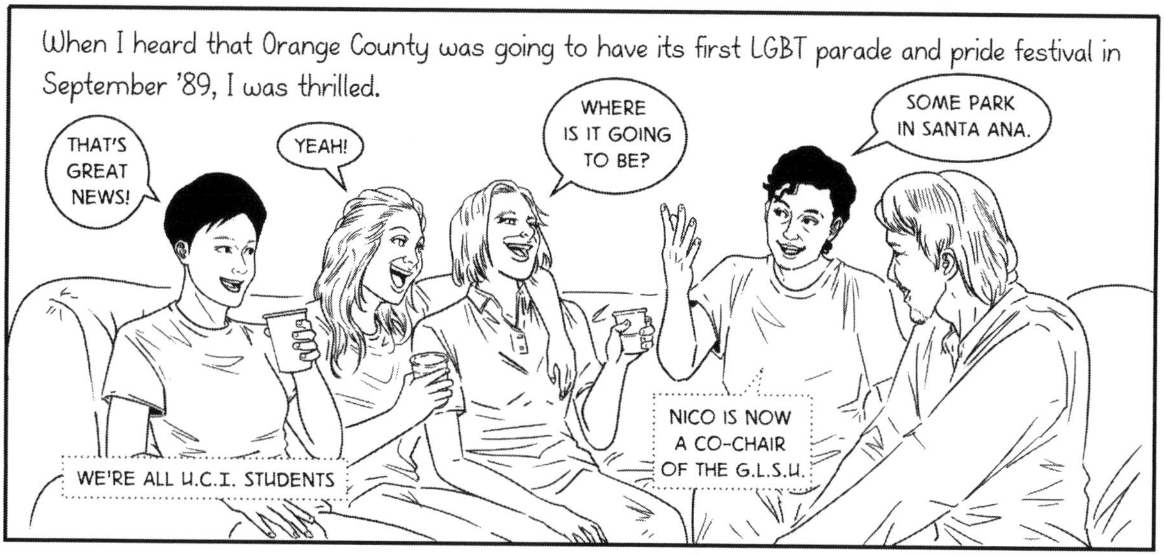
When I heard that Orange County was going to have its first LGBT parade and pride festival in September '89, I was thrilled.
THAT'S GREAT NEWS!
YEAH!
WHERE IS IT GOING TO BE?
SOME PARK IN SANTA ANA.
WE'RE ALL U.C.I. STUDENTS
NICO IS NOW A CO-CHAIR OF THE G.L.S.U.

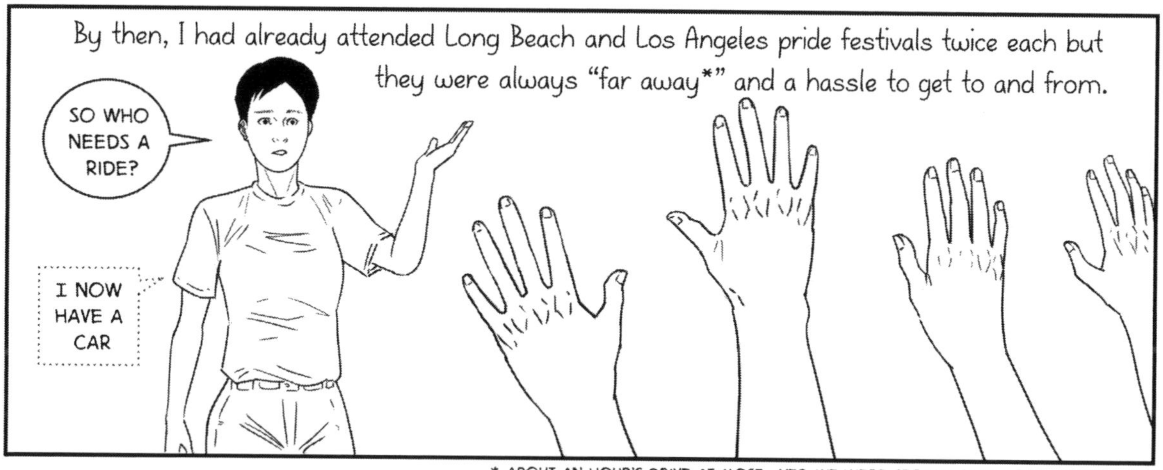
By then, I had already attended Long Beach and Los Angeles pride festivals twice each but they were always "far away*" and a hassle to get to and from.
SO WHO NEEDS A RIDE?
I NOW HAVE A CAR

* ABOUT AN HOUR'S DRIVE AT MOST. YES, WE WERE SPOILED SOUTHERN CALIFORNIANS.

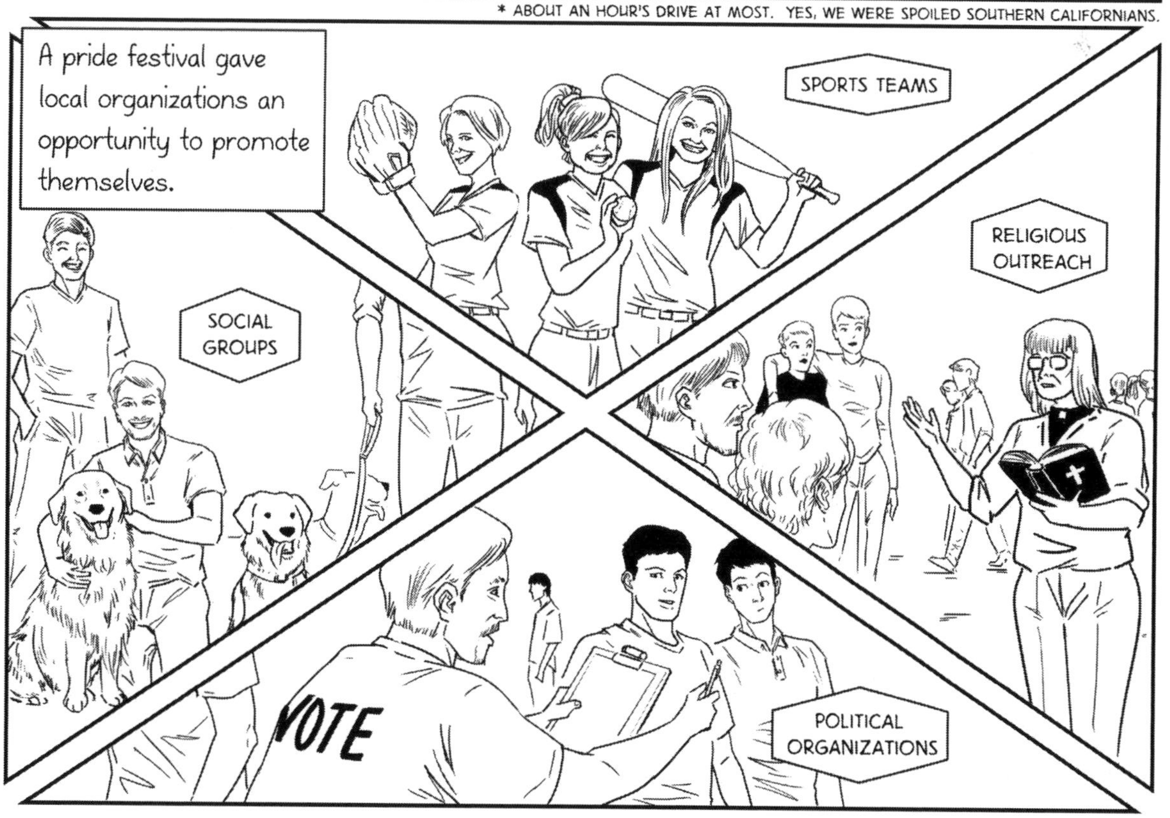
A pride festival gave local organizations an opportunity to promote themselves.
SPORTS TEAMS
RELIGIOUS OUTREACH
SOCIAL GROUPS
VOTE
POLITICAL ORGANIZATIONS

However, when we heard that the official name of the festival was "Orange County Cultural Pride," we felt that name was too closeted. Many of us expected at least the word 'gay' in the name.

"O.C.C.P.?"

I GUESS.

I found out a couple of years later that the non-queer name was purposefully chosen for the expected negative publicity.

IT GAVE US GROUNDS FOR TAKING LEGAL ACTION IF A VENDOR SUDDENLY REFUSED TO DO BUSINESS WITH US BECAUSE THEY FOUND OUT WE WERE A GAY ORGANIZATION.

But for those of us who still felt such precautions were a bad example, it was pointed out that the Los Angeles gay & lesbian pride organization is officially named "Christopher Street West."

CSW
CHRISTOPHER STREET WEST
PRESENTS

LOS ANGELES
GAY & LESBIAN
PRIDE

Well, you can't argue with such a precedent.

So when the O.C.C.P. representative applied for parade and festival permits at the Santa Ana City Hall, the permits were granted without fuss.

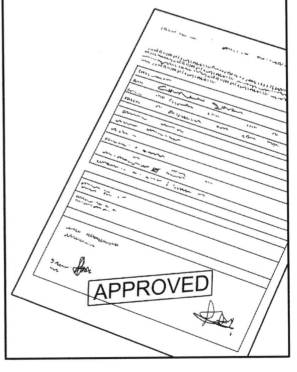

APPROVED

With OCCP scheduled the week before the start of the school year, the UCI GLSU didn't decide on any formal activities for the event because we would be preparing for orientation week.

Making our individual plans, we relied on seeing each other at some point during pride weekend.

Back then I believed in supporting the festival by attending both days. Saturday was expected to be quiet and relaxed because Sunday was the day of the parade, which always drew more attendees.

Yes, there were protestors outside on Saturday but we ignored them, as you learn to do when you attend these types of events.

So my friends and I had a great but low key time on Saturday, enjoying the people and booths of organizations based in Orange County.

On Sunday, I drove us there early in the morning so we could get a decent spot for my car in the parking lot and for ourselves on the parade route.

LOOK!

SODOMITES OUT OF SANTA ANA!

It was then we got our first literal sign of how the day would go.

SODOMITES OUT OF SANTA ANA!

Ignoring the spectacle above, we looked for a spot to sit and watch the parade.

I don't remember whose decision it was, but we ultimately ended up sitting right across from the parade protestors.

This was the first time that I really took a look at who was against this event and people like me.

I had seen pride protestors before, and they were subjects of annoyance and derision, easy to push out of your mind once they were out of sight.

REPENT! SINNERS

GOD HATES GAYS

YE MUST BE BORN AGAIN

STANDARD BUNCH OF PROTESTORS FROM OTHER FESTIVALS

But the group protesting OCCP was VERY different from the other protestor crowds...

Orange County is nicknamed "The Orange Curtain" because of the large proportion of registered Republicans and for being the home of high profile mega churches.

As expected by the OCCP organizers, the approved permits quickly came to the attention of ultra-conservative politicians and religious leaders, who were instantly horrified by such an event.

These leaders applied political pressure to the Santa Ana City Council to add the revocation of the OCCP permits to their next meeting. Supporters of both sides would attend to debate the issue before the city council vote.

So many people showed up that the overflow crowd was forced to wait in the courtyard.

The pride supporters were not even allowed in the council chambers. The mayor determined that the only speaker allowed on behalf of OCCP (and the only official gay person) would be their attorney, John Duran.

My friend Joseph Amster wanted to attend the meeting as a supporter for OCCP but was forced to wait with the overflow out in the courtyard.

Without clear territorial lines, people who were there to support (or protest) both sides of the issues were forced to pass the time side by side, doing what they felt was important for the issue at hand: debating, arguing or praying.

Being a long-time activist himself with years of public protesting experience, Joseph had never seen a gathering with such crazy, close-quarters dynamics, before or since.

Meanwhile, within the city council chamber, a variety of people testified for revocation of OCCP's permits by stating their views of queer people.

THEY'RE WICKED!

EVIL!

CHILD MOLESTERS!

MENTALLY ILL!

PERVERTS!

As the lone voice for OCCP (and the Orange County LGBT community), John Duran had the burden to counter-act this legally sanctioned name-calling.

THE *FIRST AMENDMENT* PROTECTS FREEDOM OF SPEECH AND FREEDOM OF ASSEMBLY.

IF THE CITY COUNCIL *REVOKES* THE PERMIT, IT WOULD *VIOLATE* THE *U.S. CONSTITUTION!*

He was apparently successful since the city council voted 4 to 3 to allow the permits to stay.

The reaction was obvious.

O.C.C.P. WON!

YES!!!

YES!!!

NO!!!

NO!!!

NO!!!

YES!!!

John had to be escorted out because the fundamentalists were trying to exorcise him.

The loss at the city council meeting lead to the idea of a massive protest at the pride parade, the festival's key event.

It was obvious that most had never protested a pride event before, making it a full family day activity by showing their own family-values with diversity from grandparents to grandchildren.

Joseph told me later that there were reports of nails in the parking lot and dirty diapers thrown at festival attendees

Nico was there with his boyfriend, who studied gays and Christianity and also found the protestors "fascinating."

His boyfriend wanted to take a closer look at the protestors and Nico went with him.

Nico watched a guy who looked like he could be his uncle ranting about deviants from Los Angeles and San Francisco coming into O.C. and spreading their corruption.

YOU DON'T BELONG IN ORANGE COUNTY!

It was as if the man couldn't accept the idea that queers actually existed in O.C., an attitude shared by other protestors.

I was personally horrified that the protestors involved their children, who clearly had no idea or care about what was going on.

HI!

HI!

I decided to keep an eye on them as the morning progressed.

And so the parade proceeded through this tiny space of very emotional people.

The parade participants understood the strangeness of the situation as they wanted to thank us for our support...

... and to show the protestors what they thought of them.

The most memorable moment for me was when the float for a lesbian bar came down the route and blasted Madonna's "Burning Up", which drowned out any noise from the protestors, a welcomed break for those of us sitting across from them all morning.

The children of the protestors were swept up in the fun and music of the moment too.

Their parents weren't happy about it.

As the parade neared its end, my friends and I decided to beat the crowd by heading for the festival grounds.

However, we were back inside for only a few minutes before:

ALL FESTIVAL ATTENDEES, PLEASE GATHER IN FRONT OF THE MAIN STAGE NOW!

Since many people were still out watching the parade, we were quickly assembled and they ordered us sit down on the grass.
Of course, we were all confused and curious about this unusual request.

They then announced that a **disturbance** happened at the parade and that there are discussions going on if the festival would be shut down because of it.

Nico was caught in the crowds outside the festival entrance, not sure if they would be allowed in.

Joseph noticed that policemen in riot gear and on horseback were ominously patrolling the festival fence while watching us carefully, a sign of the seriousness of the situation.

We would all find out later that the riot started because members of Act-UP L.A. and the Orange County Visibility League did a kiss-in right in front of the group of protestors.*

* MY FRIENDS AND I MISSED THIS INTERACTION BY MINUTES.

The protestors reacted as expected.

The riot ready police intervened, arresting six people, which provided front page photos for the major newspapers in the area. The confrontation lasted only a few minutes.

After peace was restored, the chief of police of Santa Ana and Attorney John Duran* debated the future of the festival. A fundamentalist leader gave his unsurprising opinion on the matter.

I'M **SHUTTING DOWN** THE FESTIVAL!

DO IT!

NO, YOU'RE **NOT!**

YOU ALREADY RESTORED ORDER!

* HE WAS THE FESTIVAL'S MAN OF THE YEAR.

BACK OFF OR I'LL **ARREST YOU** TOO!

THEN WE'LL SLAP YOU WITH A **LAWSUIT** SO YOU BETTER GET ADVICE FROM THE CITY ATTORNEY BEFORE YOU COST SANTA ANA **MILLIONS OF DOLLARS!**

So the police chief actually called the city attorney, who agreed with John.

The festival would go on!

36

When it was announced that the festival would NOT be cancelled, we cheered and quickly got back to doing what we were doing before: having fun.

OCCP's story was hardly finished, as the struggle for acceptance by both the queer attendees and our neighbors continued for several years. Due to lack of interest from the LGBT community, the festival had to shut down over a decade later.

There would be more attempts to bring pride festivals and parades back to Orange County, the most recent attempt being 2016.

But that day made an impact on all of us who were there, knowing that we were part of history in our own way and we couldn't help but feel triumphant.

For me personally, having been completely caught off guard by all of the weekend's drama, it was my first true exposure to the struggles of LGBT activism in the greater community, outside the bubble of campus life. And perhaps it whet my appetite for things to come.

– END –

Mind Games

Story: P. Kristen Enos – Art: Casandra Grullon

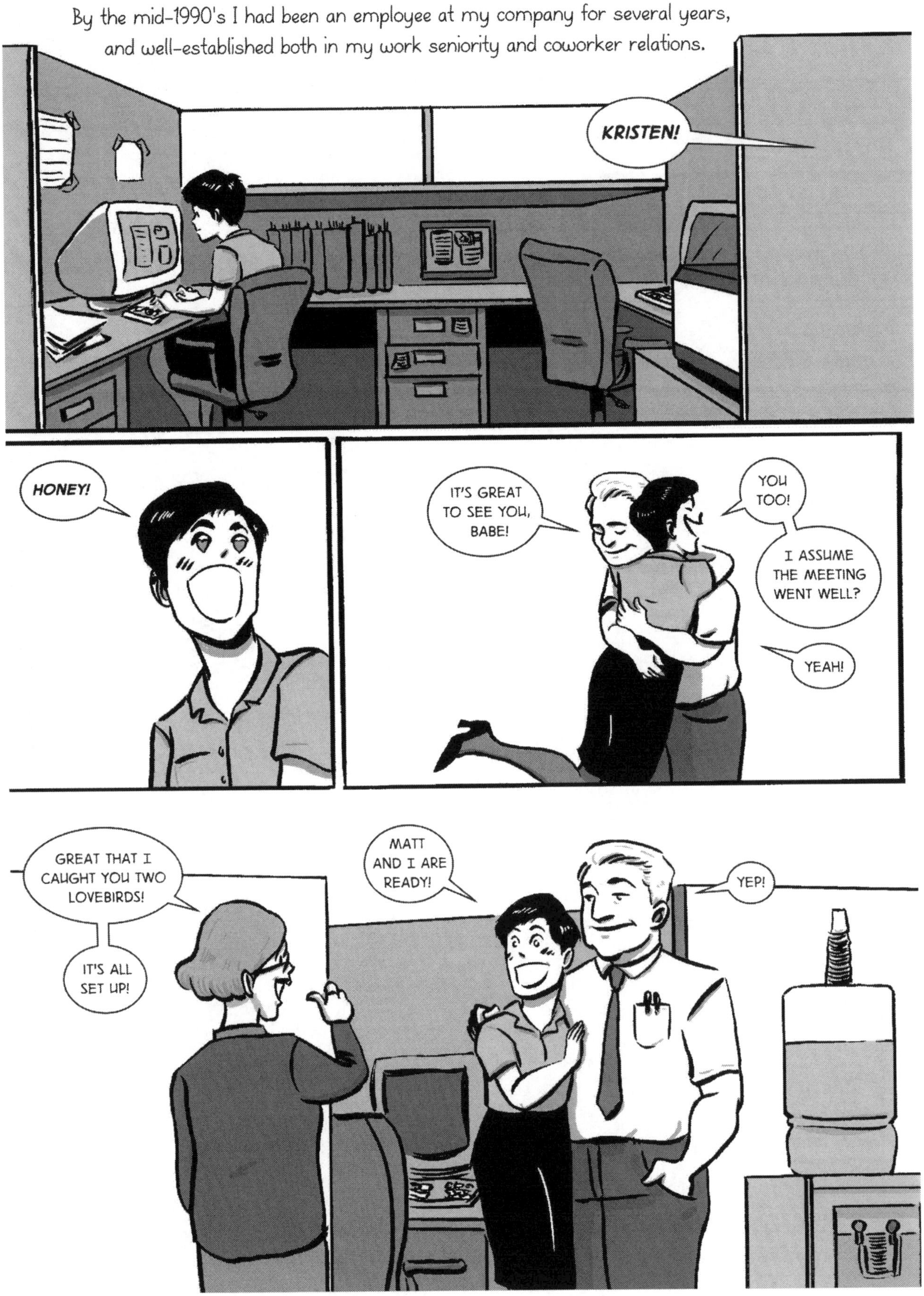
By the mid-1990's I had been an employee at my company for several years, and well-established both in my work seniority and coworker relations.
KRISTEN!
HONEY!
IT'S GREAT TO SEE YOU, BABE!
YOU TOO!
I ASSUME THE MEETING WENT WELL?
YEAH!
GREAT THAT I CAUGHT YOU TWO LOVEBIRDS!
IT'S ALL SET UP!
MATT AND I ARE READY!
YEP!

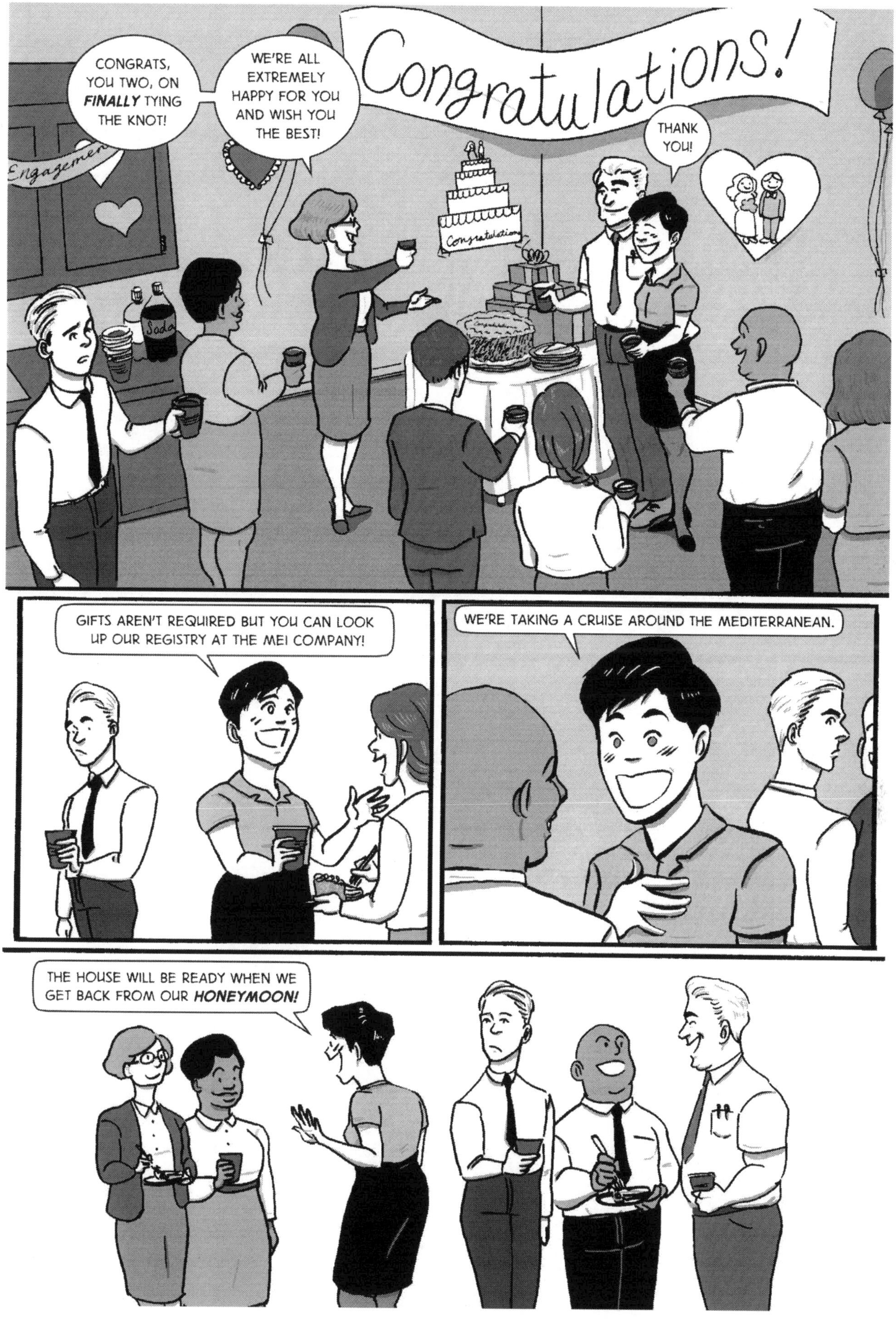
CONGRATS, YOU TWO, ON **FINALLY** TYING THE KNOT!
WE'RE ALL EXTREMELY HAPPY FOR YOU AND WISH YOU THE BEST!
Congratulations!
THANK YOU!
GIFTS AREN'T REQUIRED BUT YOU CAN LOOK UP OUR REGISTRY AT THE MEI COMPANY!
WE'RE TAKING A CRUISE AROUND THE MEDITERRANEAN.
THE HOUSE WILL BE READY WHEN WE GET BACK FROM OUR **HONEYMOON!**

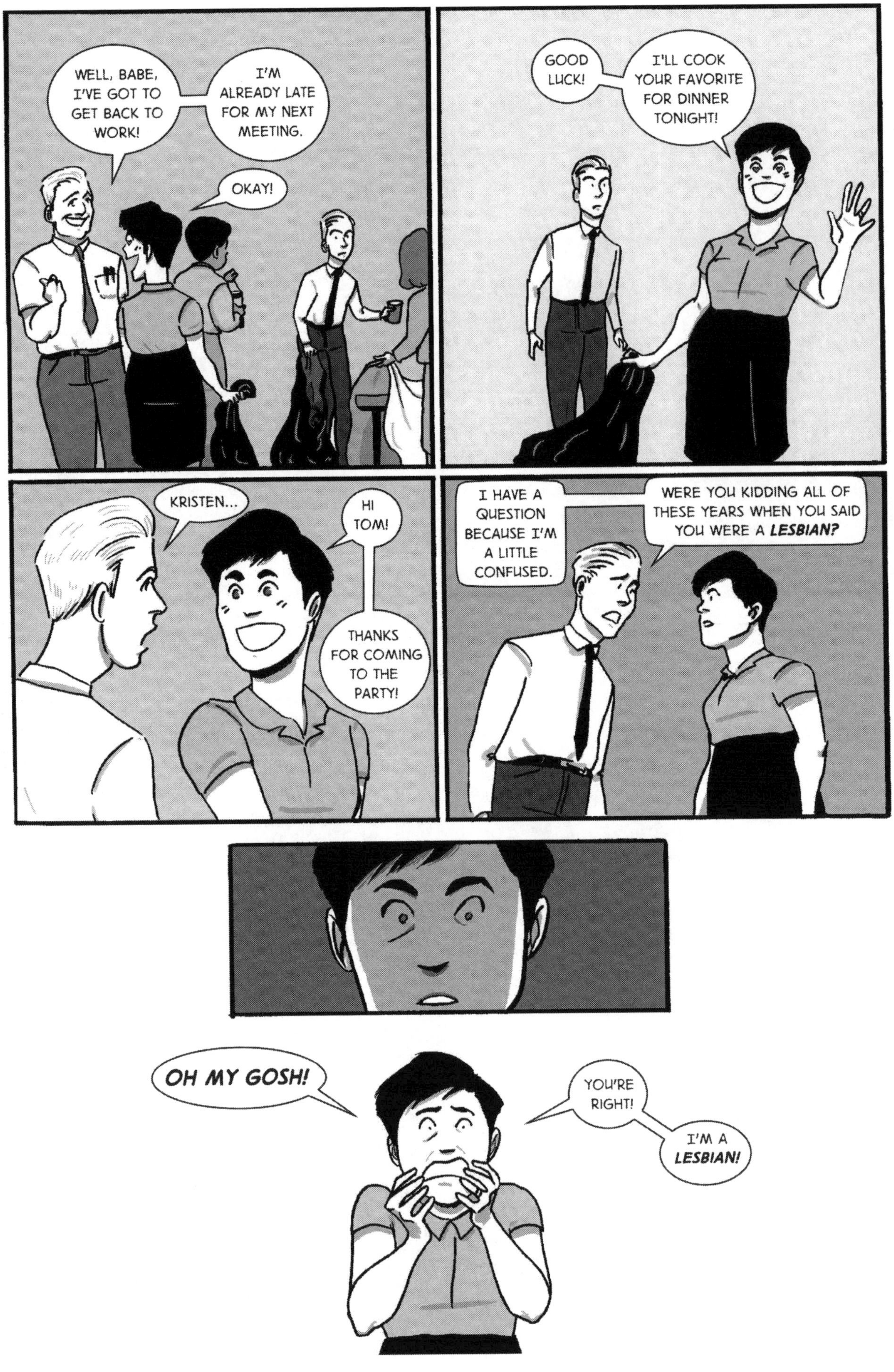
WELL, BABE, I'VE GOT TO GET BACK TO WORK!
I'M ALREADY LATE FOR MY NEXT MEETING.
OKAY!
GOOD LUCK!
I'LL COOK YOUR FAVORITE FOR DINNER TONIGHT!
KRISTEN...
HI TOM!
THANKS FOR COMING TO THE PARTY!
I HAVE A QUESTION BECAUSE I'M A LITTLE CONFUSED.
WERE YOU KIDDING ALL OF THESE YEARS WHEN YOU SAID YOU WERE A *LESBIAN?*
OH MY GOSH!
YOU'RE RIGHT!
I'M A *LESBIAN!*

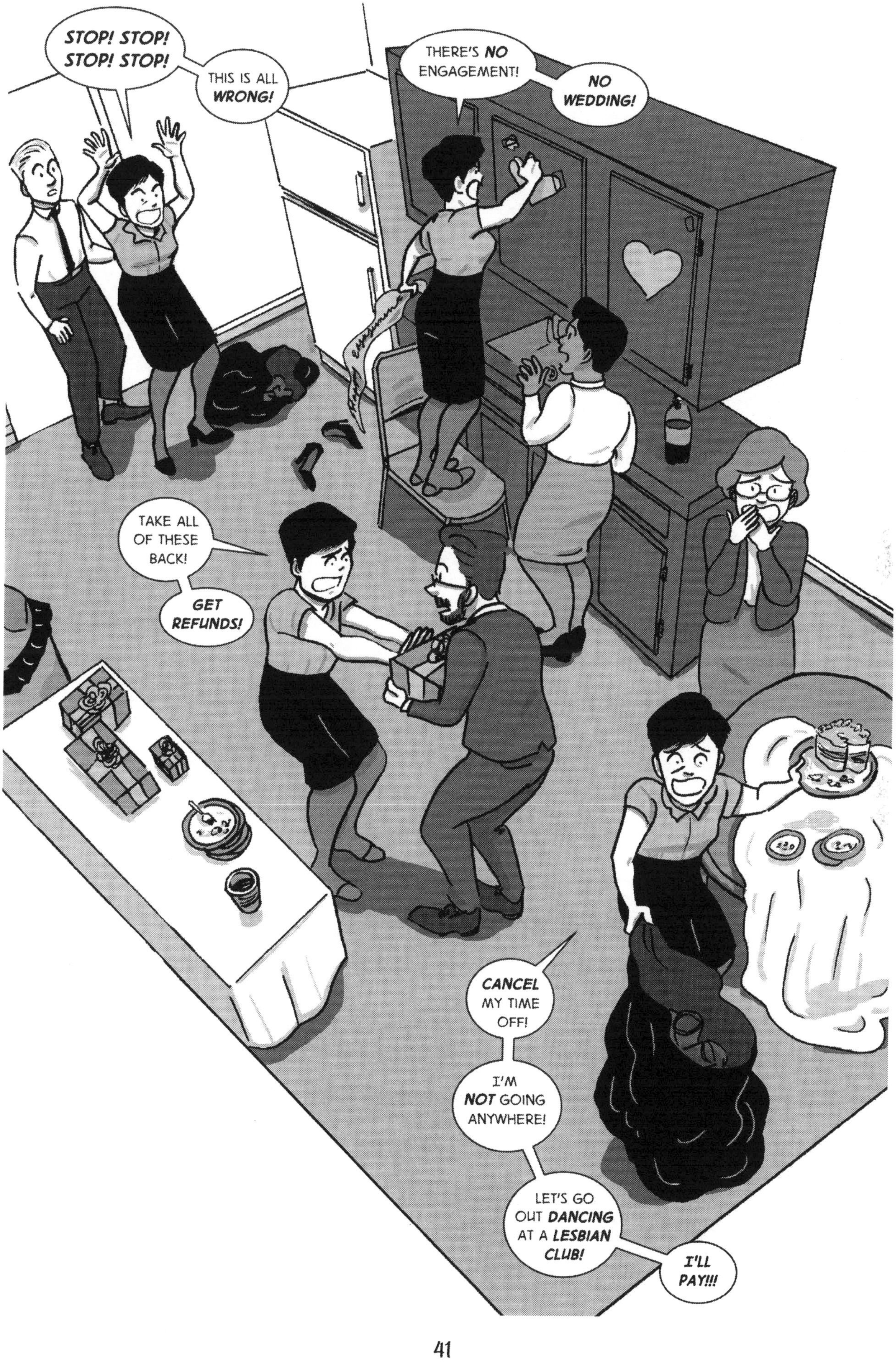
STOP! STOP! STOP! STOP!
THIS IS ALL WRONG!
THERE'S NO ENGAGEMENT!
NO WEDDING!
TAKE ALL OF THESE BACK!
GET REFUNDS!
CANCEL MY TIME OFF!
I'M NOT GOING ANYWHERE!
LET'S GO OUT DANCING AT A LESBIAN CLUB!
I'LL PAY!!!

MAKING SURE THE DREAM IS REALLY OVER.

WHEW!

Of course I HAD to tell my coworker friends about the dream the very next day. We all had a really good laugh over it.

One coworker was amazed that I would try to change the events in my own dream.

That observation was interesting to me.

I had had a previous dream where I was pregnant and I spent my time trying to find a back alley abortion.

Yes, you could call that one a TRUE NIGHTMARE.

As a psych major in college, I felt comfortable with the idea of dreams being symbolic more than literal. Especially *that* one.

While I don't have that many dreams, I can't remember any where I remained passive about unpleasant events.

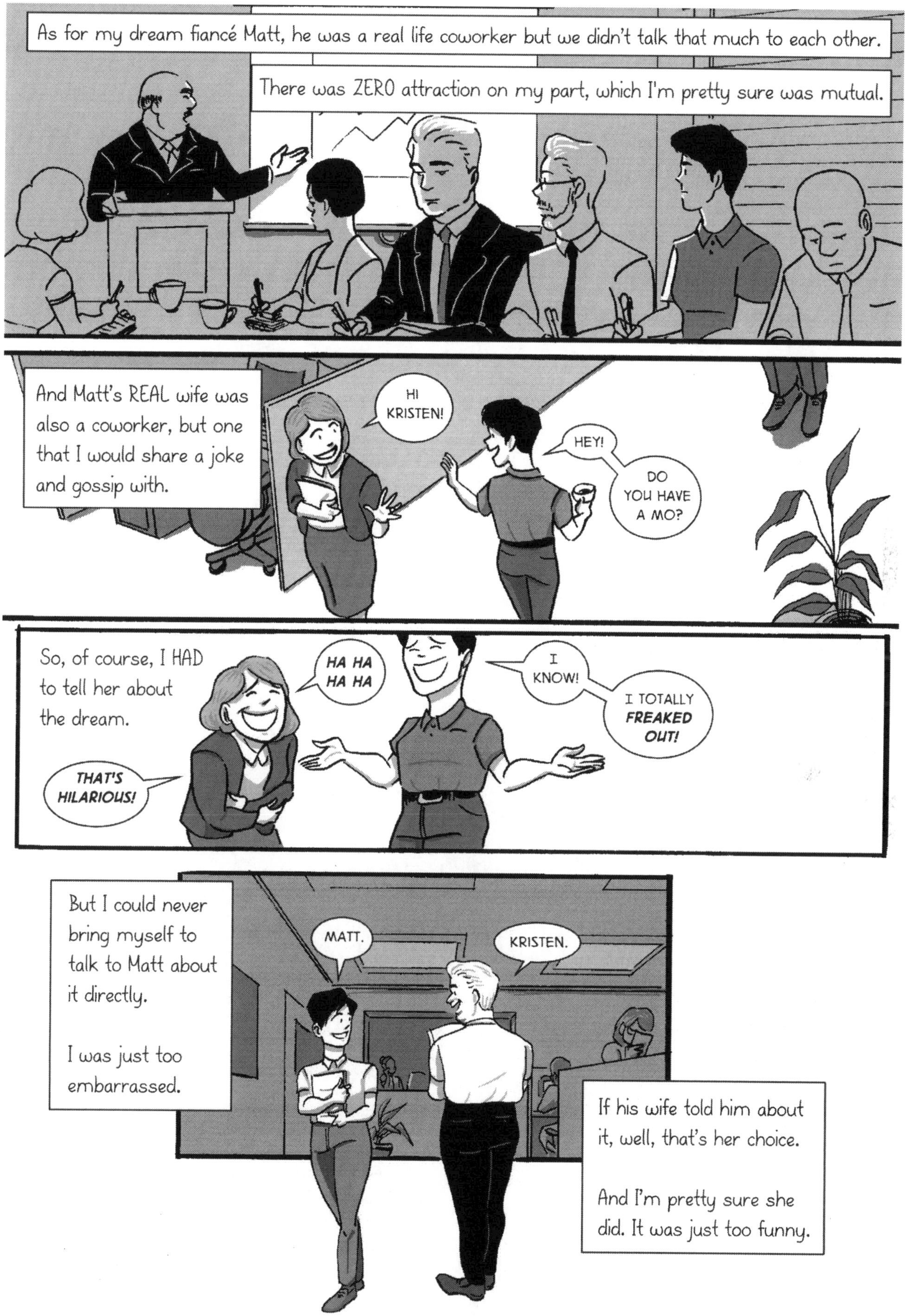
As for my dream fiancé Matt, he was a real life coworker but we didn't talk that much to each other.
There was ZERO attraction on my part, which I'm pretty sure was mutual.
And Matt's REAL wife was also a coworker, but one that I would share a joke and gossip with.
HI KRISTEN!
HEY!
DO YOU HAVE A MO?
So, of course, I HAD to tell her about the dream.
HA HA HA HA
I KNOW!
I TOTALLY FREAKED OUT!
THAT'S HILARIOUS!
But I could never bring myself to talk to Matt about it directly.
I was just too embarrassed.
MATT.
KRISTEN.
If his wife told him about it, well, that's her choice.
And I'm pretty sure she did. It was just too funny.

– END –

Story: P. Kristen Enos - Art: Leesamarie Croal

If I were to choose a single label for myself, it would be "writer," of both fiction and non-fiction since I was in elementary school.

Being a strong-willed child (and then adult), I've had a life-long, deeply-passionate dislike for censorship, whether written or verbal.

I didn't like being told that I should be quiet or having my words dismissed.

Also, don't try to keep info *from* me, being a child with an extremely curious mind,

I don't even know what kind of person I would have become had the internet been available when I was child.

I was mischievous enough without it.

*Predictably, when I was old enough to see the film on my own, I lost all interest.

I respected people who were honest with me, no matter how surprising or ugly it could be.

12TH GRADE

SHE DIDN'T BELIEVE THE HOLOCAUST HAPPENED.*

The point of such moments is to have two-way communication and to reach an understanding.

NOT HER REAL REACTION BUT PRETTY CLOSE.

Even if it means ending in agreeing to disagree.

*At the time, I didn't know there were people like that.

I'm hardly naïve about how much words can hurt since I've had my fair share hurled at me.

ASIAN-AMERICAN IN THE '70'S

BUTCH HAIR AND FASHION SENSE

STRONG-WILLED AND VOCAL GIRL WHEN THE ADULTS IN MY CHILDHOOD WERE **NOT** FEMINISTS

These acts of negativity fed my desire for social justice as a lesbian feminist activist.

So it wasn't that surprising that I became one of the Co-Chairs of the Gay and Lesbian Student Union (GLSU) at University of California, Irvine (UCI) in the early '90s.

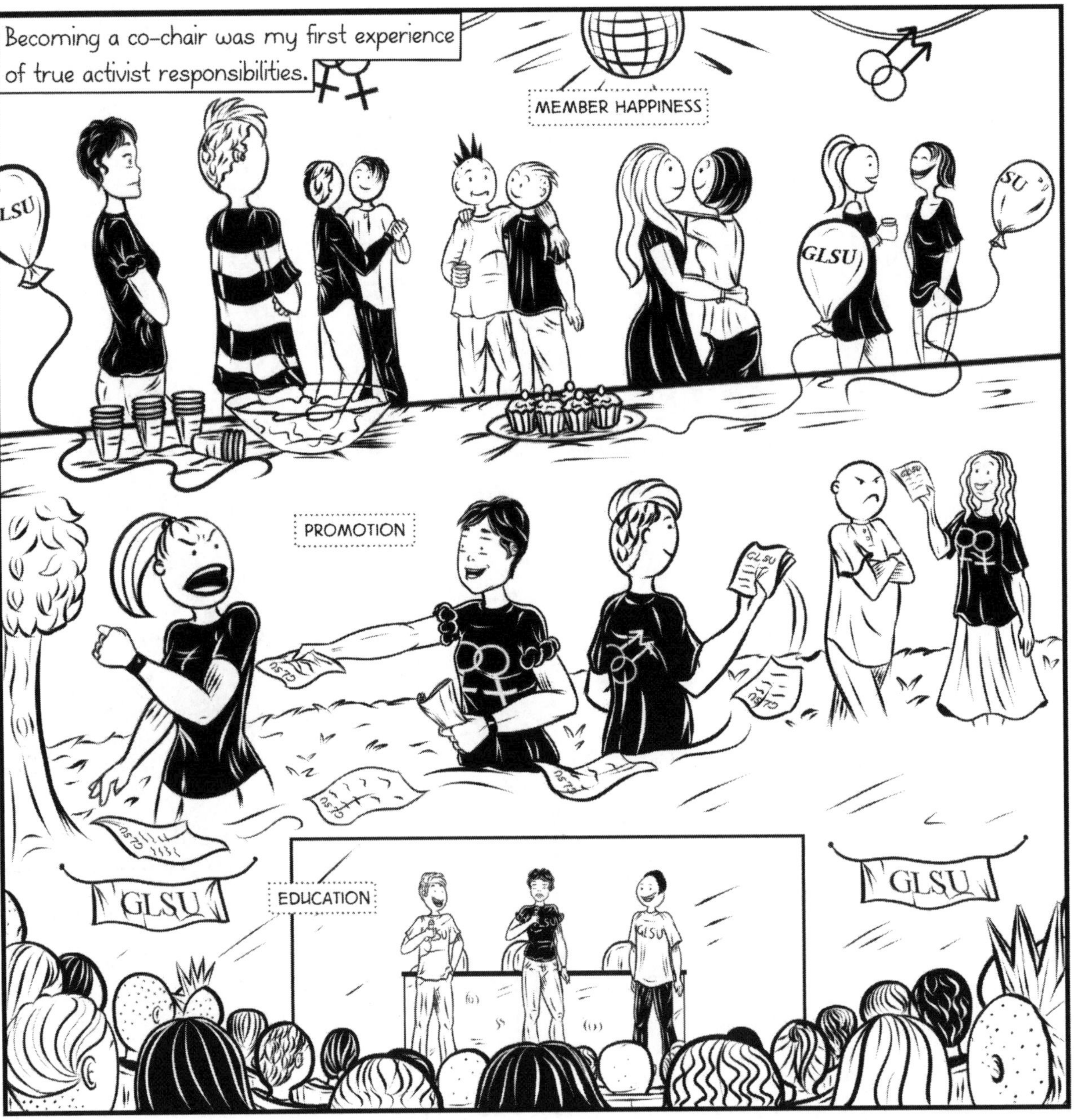
Becoming a co-chair was my first experience of true activist responsibilities.
MEMBER HAPPINESS
GLSU
GLSU
SU
PROMOTION
GLSU
EDUCATION
GLSU
GLSU

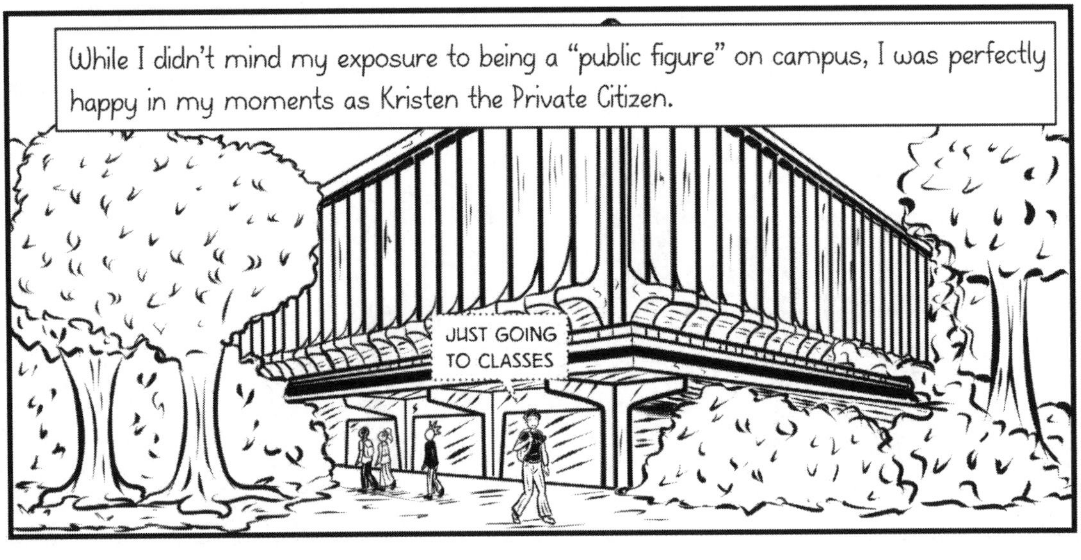
While I didn't mind my exposure to being a "public figure" on campus, I was perfectly happy in my moments as Kristen the Private Citizen.
JUST GOING TO CLASSES

It was during one of those moments that I noticed something unpleasant.

Student organizations used the walking bridges to promote their events, whether with flyers or crudely made banners.

I normally didn't pay attention to these posters unless I was keeping an eye out for our GLSU fliers or banners that may have been ripped down, but this one caught my eye.

Come Join Our Sports Club! We're Looking For Real MEN!

THE "NO FAIRIES" SYMBOLISM WAS A RED FLAG TO ME

In the spirit of free speech, I respected their right to tell the world how stupid they were, so Private Citizen Kristen would have just rolled her eyes and walked on. But I realized Activist Kristen should act differently.

Plus, I don't agree with the idea of insulting people as a recruiting tactic.

I knew I had to act on behalf of students who would be hurt by this idiotic and childish "joke."

The real question was "What Do I Do?"

Without cell phones or social media, I didn't have any friends to bounce ideas off of.

And as a person who was bullied in junior high, I know all options are complicated.

But I knew I had to act as soon as possible.

I didn't want to rip down the banner because I didn't want it to be replaced by something just as bad or worse.

And I didn't know how many of these posters were around campus.

And confronting the sports team* directly could easily escalate into ugliness.

*DISCLAIMER: NO, IT WAS NOT THE BASEBALL TEAM THAT CREATED THE BANNER. THIS IMAGE WAS JUST AS AN EXAMPLE.

I realized the option to try first was going to the UCI equivalent of calling on mom or dad.

ADMINISTRATION BUILDING

I wasn't exactly sure who could help in university administration, but I knew asking was better than nothing.

POINTING ME TO THE OMBUDSMAN AS SOMEONE WHO WOULD DEAL WITH STUDENT COMPLAINTS.

I was glad that the ombudsman reacted appropriately to my view of the situation.

LOOK, I DON'T WANT TO MAKE TROUBLE *BUT...*

She assured me that she would address it right away and report back.

So I left with the feeling that I had done the right thing for that moment.

The next day I walked by that bridge and the offending poster had been taken down.

The ombudsman told me that she met with the sports team's leader and they just thought it was a funny poster, so she educated them that it wasn't.

I don't know if the sports team members really understood the issue, but I never saw another student-made poster like that again in my years at UCI.

– END –

I had worked with the same company for over twenty five years. I liked working for such a large corporation because company policies dictated respect and protection for employees based on such criteria as gender, race and, yes, sexual orientation... which all applied to me.

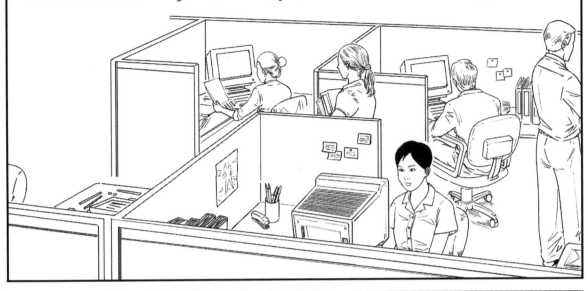

Because you spend several hours a day with your coworkers, you should be mature and respectful adults about your personal differences in order to do your jobs.

While I was openly lesbian, I knew there were people who clearly weren't hooked into the "Kristen Is A Dyke" rumor mill.

FIRST STACY AND THEN KATHY. WITH ALL OF THESE UNEXPECTED PREGNANCIES, KRISTEN, YOU SHOULD BE CAREFUL.

NOT REALLY MY CONCERN, JANE.

OH, YOU NEVER KNOW!*

*Well, yes, it was POSSIBLE that I could trip and fall on a sperm-filled turkey baster, but I still wasn't worried.

But I admit there had been a few moments of crossing that line of corporate pleasantries. For example: in 1997, we had a woman, Kirsten, transfer from our Bellevue, WA office to my team based in Irvine, CA.

HER HUSBAND ALSO WORKED FOR THE COMPANY AND HAD ALREADY TRANSFERRED TO THE IRVINE OFFICE.

To welcome her to the team, our supervisor Patty thought introductions in the next staff meeting would be appropriate.

For teammates who were out or in other meetings, we take notes, so I volunteered.

NOT BROWN-NOSING, JUST WANTING TO GET MY TURN OVER WITH.

What I didn't know was that Rose the Admin was on the agenda for giving a speech, something that had never happened before.

I had only been with the team for about a year or two and my prior interactions with Rose the Admin were strictly business related.

THE COPIER IS OUT OF TONER AGAIN.

OKAY. I'LL TAKE CARE OF IT.

While I never asked about her, I somehow knew that Rose had been with the company for over thirty years. She used to be a telephone pole technician, something she was rightfully proud of.

THIS PART OF HER I RESPECTED

⭐ ⭐ ⭐ VOTE ⭐ ⭐ ⭐
REPUBLICAN

However her cube decorations, especially around election time, warned me to steer clear of personal discussions with her.

THIS PART OF HER I DIDN'T

While I'm pretty sure such overt politicing was in violation of HR rules, I assumed there was some sort of blind-eye tolerance allowed given her longevity with the company.

A NEW PROJECT IS COMING...

Needless to say these concerns were in the back of my mind as I started to take notes for the meeting.

When Rose introduced her speech, my dread alert was at maximum level.

So Rose gave her speech and it was everything I feared it was going to be:

As she gave her speech, I made absolutely no pretense about how I felt about her presentation and refused to take notes.

And I didn't care what she thought of my reaction because she (and everyone else) could clearly see it.

Despite her polished language and presentation, her points were clearly the thinly veiled judgmental hate-speech that I had been used to hearing as a lesbian feminist activist.

If I had bothered to take notes, I'm sure I wouldn't have done it maturely.

"HER SPEECH WAS OFFENSIVE, IGNORANT AND HOSTILE."

When she was done, our teammates clapped. I did not even though I am normally a firm believer in good manners.

Then we did our introductions, including some personal information about ourselves.

I'M FROM BELLEVUE AND YOU ALREADY KNOW MY HUSBAND.

It just so happened that Rose's turn was before mine, and I would be last.

I USED TO CLIMB THE TELEPHONE POLES.

So it was finally my turn:

AND I'M A *LESBIAN* WHO'S A *VOTING DEMOCRAT!*

Since I wasn't looking at Rose at that moment, I don't know if this was her expression but I'm pretty sure it was close. And at that moment I honestly didn't care if I alienated other team members.

Just like with other introductions, our team politely clapped, ending the meeting.

Because I had a practice of coming out to my supervisors in case I should have problems with teammates, I did talk privately to Patty about how inappropriate Rose's speech was. She admitted to me that it hadn't occured to her how alienating it was because she was used to hearing those discussion points among her own friends, family and church members.

But she said would be more aware of Rose's behavior in corporate fairness. And that's all I wanted out of the conversation.

55

Rose and I never talked about that speech and my introduction, but it was clear that the vibe between us had changed.

Patty later told me Rose wanted Patty to order me to take it down my Wonder Woman picture as inappropriate.*

Patty told me that she refused Rose's request because none of my cubicle neighbors cared.

*THIS WAS BEFORE THE H.R. RULE THAT CUBICLE DECORATIONS SHOULD NOT BE SCANTILY CLAD MODELS (MALE OR FEMALE.)

Patty's admission made me realize that she had her limits with Rose as well. I also started to notice other cubicle side chats that opened my eyes to how much our teammates couldn't stand Rose's extremeness either.*

I LOVE **MESSING** WITH HER!

VOTE REPUBLICAN

* AND AFTER THAT MEETING, I NOTICED SOME TEAMMATES WERE A LOT MORE FRIENDLY TO ME AS THE RUMOR MILL WENT FULL FORCE.

Years later, Kirsten's husband admitted that she had told him about the speech and introduction the night it happened.

HAHAHA!!!

Kirsten told him it was the funniest work meeting she had ever been in, and it took all of her control to keep from bursting out in laughter.

I was pleased to know someone else thought the whole situation was unnecessarily absurd.

– END –

Story: P. Kristen Enos with Heidi Ho – Art: Casandra Grullon

A standing program sponsored by the WRC was a weekly rap group called "Above And Beyond."

Moderated by one of the WRC student staff members, the premise of the rap group was that students of all orientations could talk in a safe and supportive environment.

In 1989, it was moderated by Heidi.

PROUDLY HAWAIIAN

IDENTIFIES AS HETEROSEXUAL

She told me that she volunteered to run the program for the school year because she happened to live on campus so it was easy for her to be the "woman with the key."

I'LL DO IT!

THANKS!

My GLSU friends and I tried our best to attend.

Whether just to share experiences or ask for advice.

FOR EXAMPLE:

MODERATOR AND CURIOUS

HOW DO YOU DEAL WITH JEALOUSY WHEN YOU'RE BISEXUAL?

WELL, MY GIRLFRIEND...

In the meeting right before winter break, we discussed what we planned to do during the holidays.

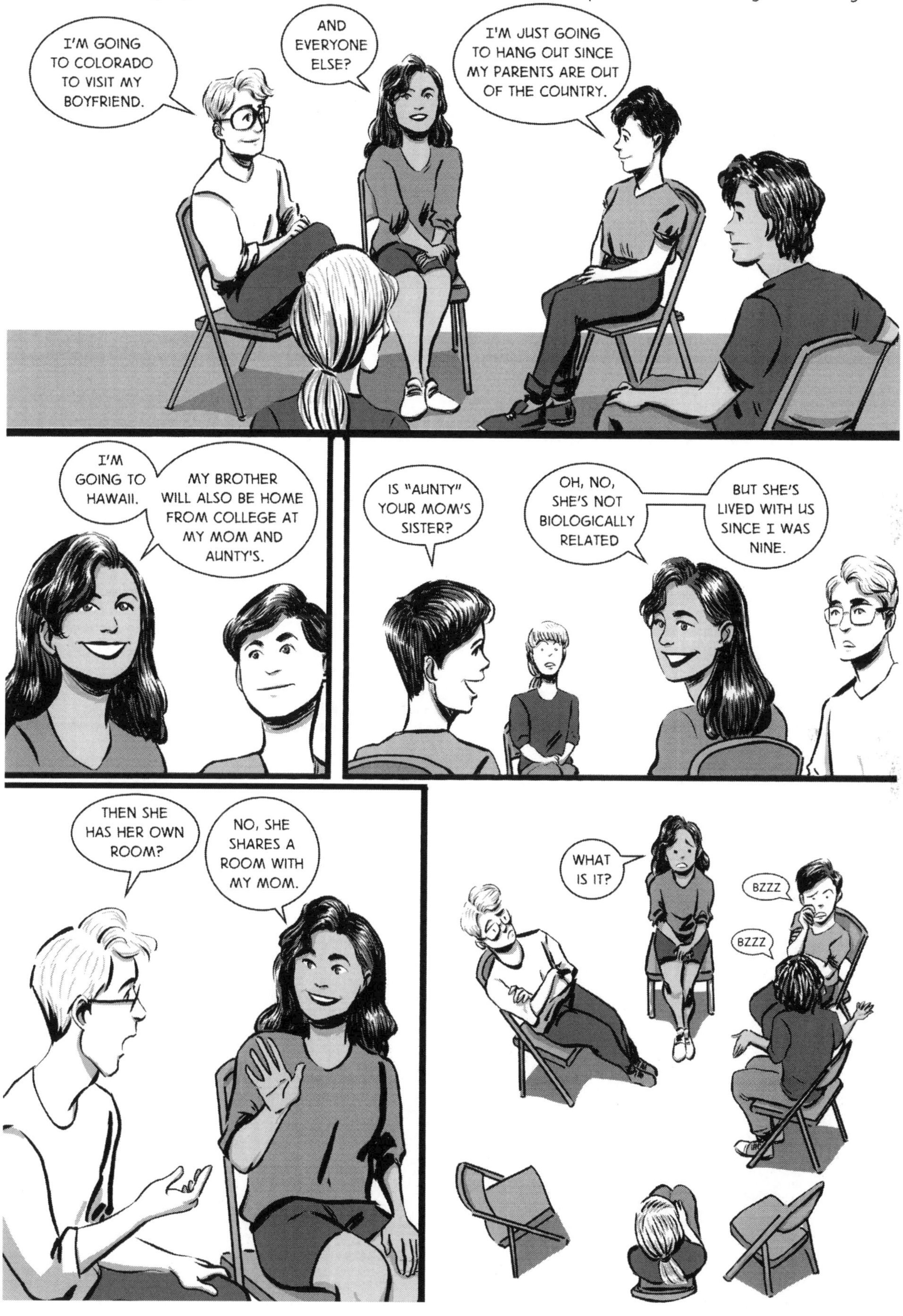
I'M GOING TO COLORADO TO VISIT MY BOYFRIEND.
AND EVERYONE ELSE?
I'M JUST GOING TO HANG OUT SINCE MY PARENTS ARE OUT OF THE COUNTRY.
I'M GOING TO HAWAII.
MY BROTHER WILL ALSO BE HOME FROM COLLEGE AT MY MOM AND AUNTY'S.
IS "AUNTY" YOUR MOM'S SISTER?
OH, NO, SHE'S NOT BIOLOGICALLY RELATED
BUT SHE'S LIVED WITH US SINCE I WAS NINE.
THEN SHE HAS HER OWN ROOM?
NO, SHE SHARES A ROOM WITH MY MOM.
WHAT IS IT?
BZZZ
BZZZ

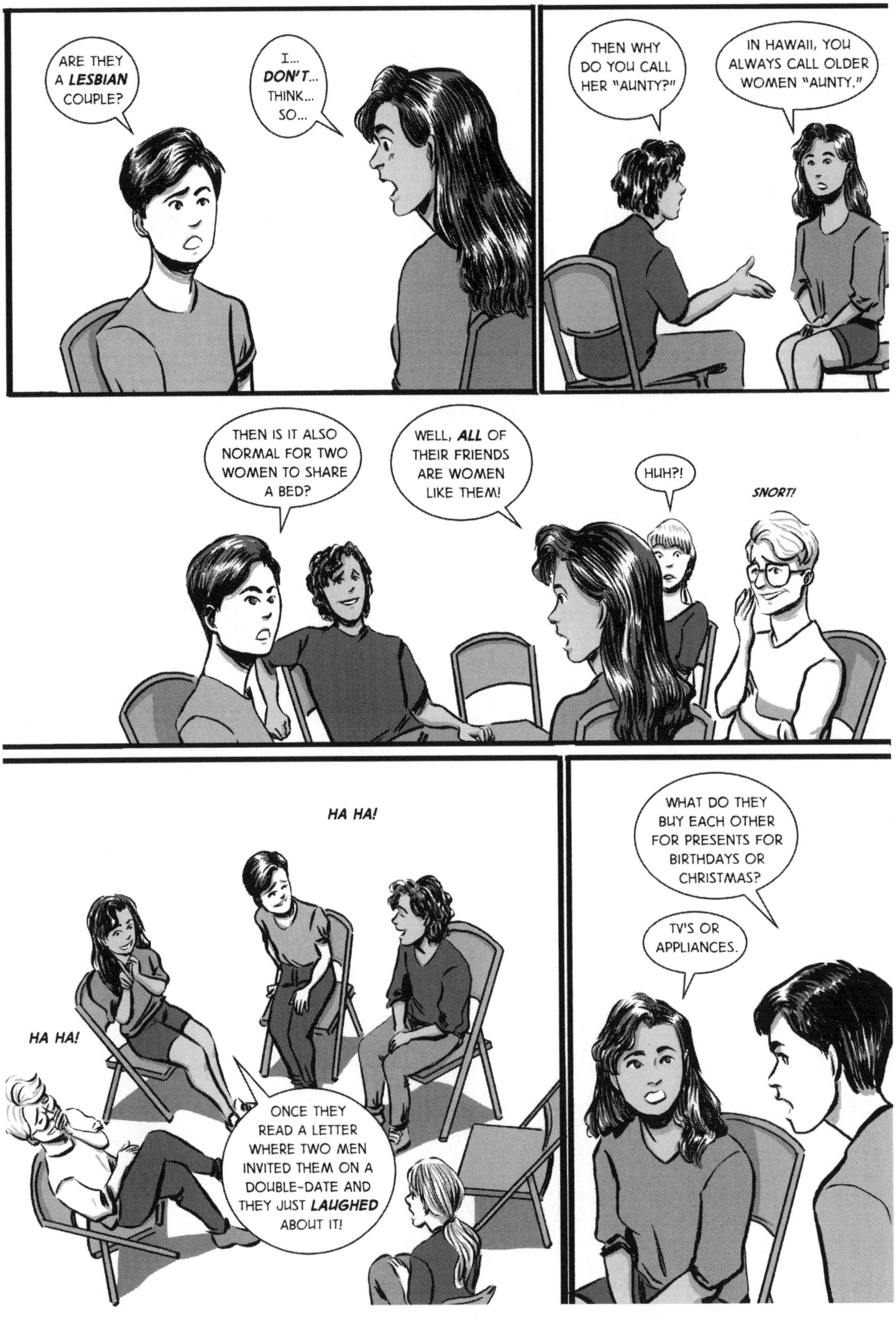
ARE THEY A **LESBIAN** COUPLE?
I... **DON'T**... THINK... SO...
THEN WHY DO YOU CALL HER "AUNTY?"
IN HAWAII, YOU ALWAYS CALL OLDER WOMEN "AUNTY."
THEN IS IT ALSO NORMAL FOR TWO WOMEN TO SHARE A BED?
WELL, **ALL** OF THEIR FRIENDS ARE WOMEN LIKE THEM!
HUH?!
SNORT!
HA HA!
HA HA!
ONCE THEY READ A LETTER WHERE TWO MEN INVITED THEM ON A DOUBLE-DATE AND THEY JUST **LAUGHED** ABOUT IT!
WHAT DO THEY BUY EACH OTHER FOR PRESENTS FOR BIRTHDAYS OR CHRISTMAS?
TV'S OR APPLIANCES.

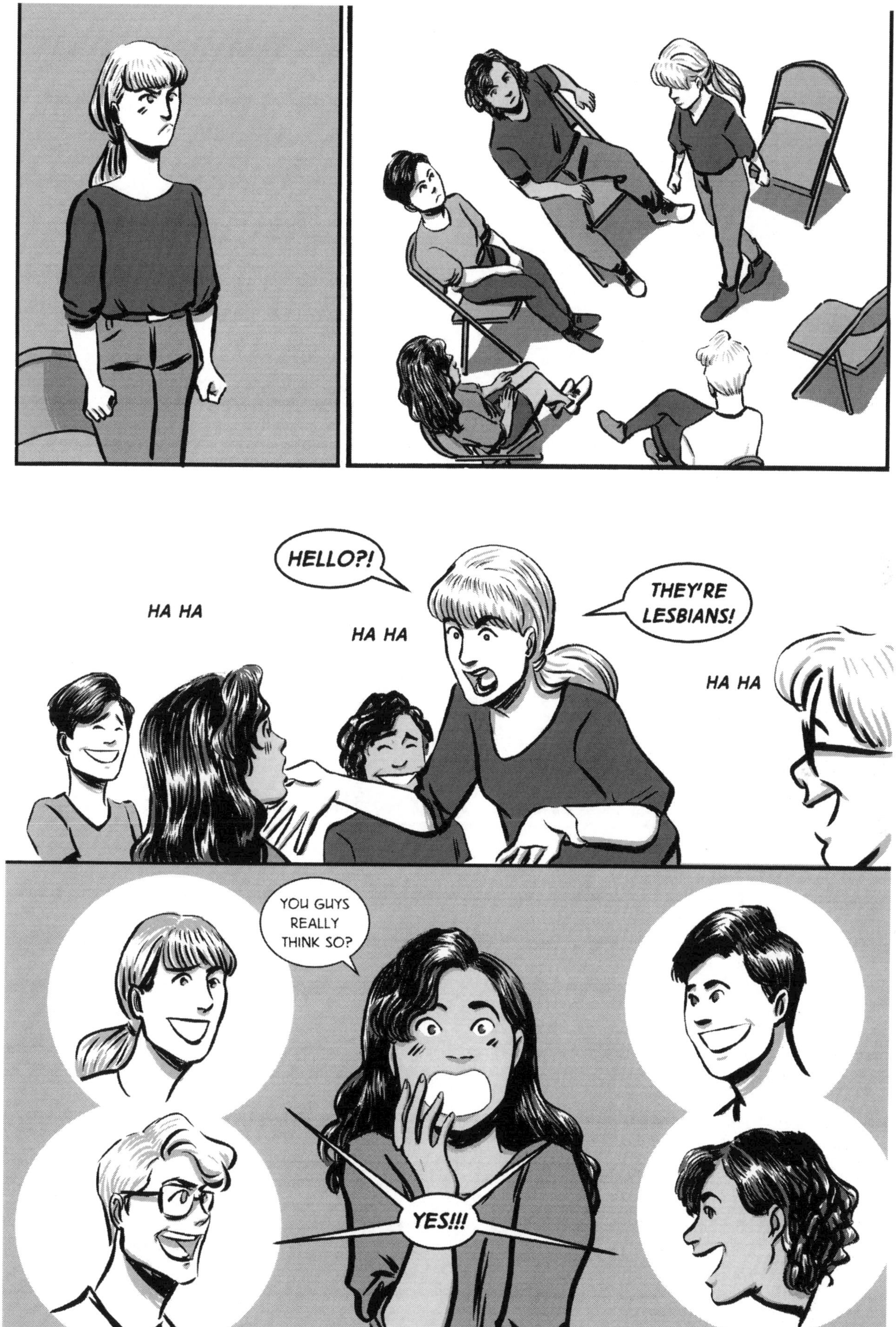
HELLO?!
HA HA
HA HA
THEY'RE LESBIANS!
HA HA
YOU GUYS REALLY THINK SO?
YES!!!

BUT THEY'VE NEVER **SAID** ANYTHING!

WELL...

SIGH

I GIVE UP!

YOU SAID YOU WANT TO BE A PRIVATE INVESTIGATOR, RIGHT?

... YES?

THEN YOU HAVE AN ASSIGNMENT TO FIND OUT IF YOUR MOM AND AUNTY ARE A LESBIAN COUPLE.

WE'LL EXPECT A REPORT IN THE FIRST MEETING AFTER WINTER BREAK.

OKAY!

ALSO GLAD THAT SHE'S NOW "COOL!"

Heidi felt very enthusiastic about the task. And with her brother, she knew that the two of them could figure it out once and for all.

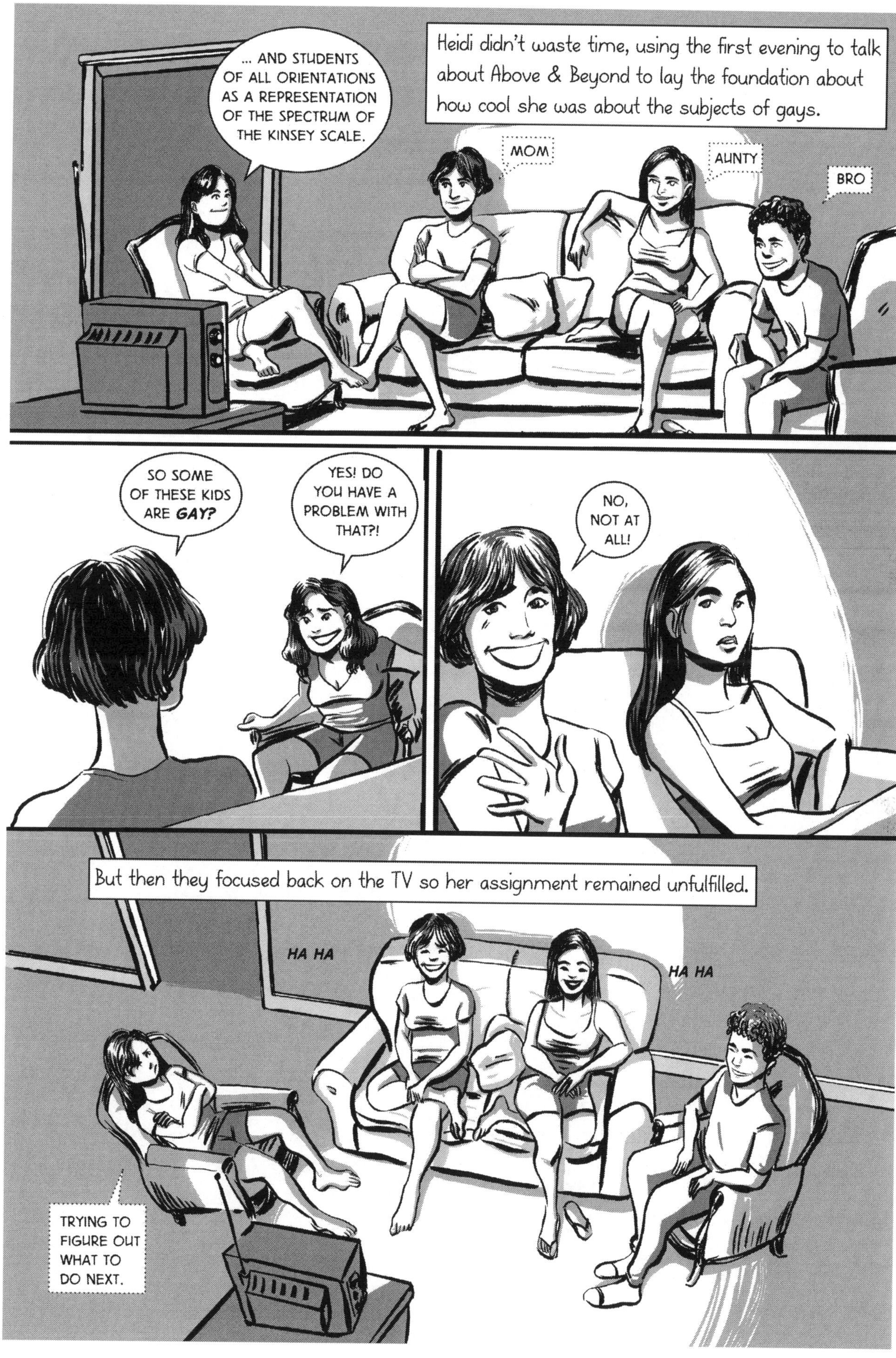
... AND STUDENTS OF ALL ORIENTATIONS AS A REPRESENTATION OF THE SPECTRUM OF THE KINSEY SCALE.
Heidi didn't waste time, using the first evening to talk about Above & Beyond to lay the foundation about how cool she was about the subjects of gays.
MOM
AUNTY
BRO
SO SOME OF THESE KIDS ARE GAY?
YES! DO YOU HAVE A PROBLEM WITH THAT?!
NO, NOT AT ALL!
But then they focused back on the TV so her assignment remained unfulfilled.
HA HA
HA HA
TRYING TO FIGURE OUT WHAT TO DO NEXT.

Later that night

HEY, DO YOU MIND GOING FOR A DRIVE?

I WANT TO TALK TO YOU ABOUT SOMETHING.

SURE.

I'LL DRIVE.

When they were on the road, Heidi decided to just let it out.

DO YOU THINK MOM AND AUNTY ARE *LESBIANS?*

His reaction:

AAA!

SQUEAL

Luckily, he recovered quickly.

Once her brother was over the initial shock, they continued to drive round and round the small island as they tried to analyze their family from a new perspective.

WHAT DO YOU THINK?

I DON'T KNOW, WHAT DO *YOU* THINK?

I ASKED YOU!

They decided that it could be likely but they didn't feel comfortable coming to a firm conclusion.

A couple of days later, Heidi decided to try her cousin.

DO YOU KNOW IF MOM AND AUNTY ARE LESBIANS?

THERE HAVE BEEN RUMORS BUT NOTHING CONFIRMED.

This cousin came out herself several years later.

Heidi still felt like she didn't have anything to help her come to a real conclusion.

And the suggestions made by those of us queer kids at the Above & Beyond meeting just weren't Heidi's style.

THEIR DOOR IS LOCKABLE.

She started to feel like her options to find out the truth were limited.

65

Feeling as if she had no more investigative options left but to be as direct as possible once she was alone with her mother:

MOM, ARE YOU *GAY?!*

DOES IT MATTER?

NO! IT DOESN'T!

THEN WHY ARE YOU ASKING?

That was her cue to give up.

NEVER MIND.

BACK TO WATCHING TV.

After winter break, she used the Above And Beyond group as a sounding board about what had happened in Hawaii.

AND THEN I ...

She seemed even more reluctant and confused about the whole matter than she was before her trip home.

We listened with the same amount of incredulousness as before.

At the end of the meeting, our positions hadn't changed:

THEY AREN'T

MAYBE?

THEY ARE!

The meeting ended with everyone going their separate ways.

WELL, YOU *TRIED*.

The conversation was memorable even if there was no closure for Heidi that night.

67

That last conversation finally clarified for me why Heidi was so reluctant to come to a firm conclusion on her own: For something this big and important, she wanted to be told directly by her mom.

She absolutely loved and respected her mom in every aspect of their lives, and honesty was part of that.

Even though I really liked this story for its uniqueness and lessons learned, I never felt comfortable writing about this incident when I had the Active Voice column in the Blade Magazine.

There were so many specific details that it felt like a breech of privacy of Heidi and her family if I couldn't get their permission and cooperation first.

I didn't think it would be possible to get their agreement in the years after college because I lost touch with her.

But then social media and robust internet search engines were invented.

When I started work on this comic collection, I did a cold internet search for Heidi and we finally reconnected.

Hi, are you Heidi Ho who ran the Above and Beyond rap group at UCI in the early 90's?

Yes, that was me!

I explained the comic project and reminded her about THAT night and wanted her permission to tell the story as an example of a loved one **WANTING** to be supportive.

I totally remember that night!

I sent her the draft of "Birth Of An Activist" as an example of how the story would be told.

Heidi gave her permission. And she got her mom's permission too!

Heidi was now happily married with teenage kids of her own (and a furry one).

Heidi's love and devotion to her mother never wavered over the years.

Heidi even told me that a year after that Above And Beyond meeting, she and her boyfriend had become serious enough to discuss marriage.

However, she hadn't yet told him about her suspicions of Mom and Aunty, which she now couldn't avoid.

So she invited him to dinner, telling him that there was something very important they needed to discuss.

Heidi knew she couldn't hold anything back that night.

LOOK, MY MOM AND AUNTY SHARE A BEDROOM WITH A LOCKABLE DOOR AND I DON'T KNOW WHAT THEIR RELATIONSHIP IS BUT I LOVE THEM BOTH DEARLY AND IF YOU HAVE A PROBLEM WITH THAT THEN I CAN'T MARRY YOU.

OH.

HAD BEEN CONVINCED THAT SHE INVITED HIM TO DINNER TO BREAK UP.

THAT'S NOT A PROBLEM AT ALL!

They've now been married for over twenty years!

As for the mystery of her mom and Aunty, Heidi said they were together for another ten years.

But when they "broke up," Heidi finally saw with clarity how intense their relationship was and had no doubts again.

Heidi told me that Aunty leaving made her feel like she was a kid watching her parents getting divorced.

When her mom became involved with Aunty #2, Heidi saw how drastically different their relationship was given that Aunty #2 was openly gay.

In fact, Aunty #2 had a grown daughter who liked to tease Heidi's mom about NOT being out.

MOM, ARE YOU CLOSETED **NOW?**

HA HA

Heidi used this revelation as her sign that she could now tease her own mom.

ARE YOU OUT **NOW?**

HA HA

OH, STOP IT!

71

Heidi said that over the years her mom did admit that at the beginning of her career, she was scared about being out.

But Heidi's mom said she eventually kept quiet to protect Heidi and her brother.

She didn't want other kids to be mean to them because of it.

Heidi's response to that:

THEN THOSE KIDS WOULDN'T HAVE BEEN MY FRIENDS.

All of this was revealed over our reunion ramen lunch.

I WAS COMPLETELY *CLUELESS* ABOUT MY MOM AND AUNTY!

YOU JUST DIDN'T HAVE GAYDAR.

We talked about why Heidi was so reluctant to label her mom during the Above & Beyond days.

I DIDN'T WANT TO LABEL MOM IF SHE WASN'T COMFORTABLE WITH THE LABEL HERSELF.

IN THAT DINNER WITH MY HUSBAND, HE TEASES ME THAT ALL I HAD TO DO WAS SAY MOM AND AUNTY WERE LESBIANS.

BUT I DIDN'T FEEL LIKE IT WAS MY RIGHT.

BACK THEN, ESPECIALLY FOR OLDER GENERATIONS, ASKING IF SOMEONE WAS GAY WAS AN INSULT.

TRUE.

WE QUEER COLLEGE KIDS WERE ALL ABOUT BEING VISIBLE AND STANDING UP FOR YOURSELF AND OTHERS.

IF YOUR MOM LIVED IN THAT ENVIRONMENT, I'M SURE SHE WOULD HAVE TOLD YOU A LONG TIME AGO.

I'D LIKE TO THINK SO, TOO.

Heidi's pride as a queer ally remains to this day.

MOM, YOU'RE SUCH A HIPSTER BECAUSE YOU WERE IN THE LGBT WORLD WAY BACK THEN!

IT WAS *ALWAYS* AN LGBT WORLD!

And I definitely agree!

– END –

73

Story: P. Kristen Enos – Art: Leesamarie Croal

It started off innocently enough.

It was the Fall of '87 and I was starting my sophomore year at UC Irvine.

Go Anteaters!

I had to buy a textbook from the campus bookstore and purposefully chose a weekend when the place would be as empty and quiet as possible.

I was walking towards the the cashier when I passed by the magazine rack and *IT* caught my eye.

A magazine cover with two women kissing in a bathtub was obviously meant to shock.

But it was beyond shocking to someone like me: a newly out lesbian who had never seen such an image before, much less on a magazine cover.

It wasn't even a "gay" magazine. And the gay mags that were there had little appeal to me.

I **HAD** to buy it, even if it meant pushing my starving college student budget.

And being before the internet, it wasn't as if I could memorize the title and try to look it up online later. It was a purchase that I needed to make NOW.

But I had never bought anything queer-related before and it was a little unnerving.

CHECKING IF ANYONE IS NEARBY

I had only recently accepted that I was a lesbian but being so public about it was not something I had had to face before.

But I felt as if I didn't have a choice.

Luckily, I realized I could hide the magazine by holding against my textbook.

Even so, I felt like I now walked through the bookstore with a big sign over me.

My nerves settled a bit as I walked through the bookstore. But they stirred again when I noticed the cashier noticing me in return.

When I realized that it was almost the moment of exposure, I did debate with myself if I should put the magazine back.

But with the bookstore so empty, I knew I would probably never have another chance to buy the magazine without anyone else noticing.

And I couldn't take the chance that the magazine would sell out.

It was then I realized that the key was just to act cool. If I don't make a big deal about it, the cashier shouldn't make a big deal out of it.

As I had hoped, once he was over the initial shock, he tried to act cool about it too.

But then the other clerk noticed my pending purchase:

And it just gets a bit worse.

My instincts took over:

They then gave me the quickest checkout experience possible.

We all clearly relaxed once my purchase was done.

Since then, my queer-related purchases have been much, much easier.

At least for me.

– END –

In my long career in the corporate world, I've been on my fair share of business trips. In 1998, I was on a work team divided into three locations of Irvine, CA; Walnut Creek, CA; and Bellevue, WA.

We were asked to attend a team meeting in San Francisco, near Walnut Creek.

BELLEVUE

WALNUT CREEK

IRVINE

We looked forward to this event that allowed us to travel on the company dollar and to hang out with coworkers who were friends.

Being a telecommunications company, we perfected the art of working "virtually" over the phone and internet, but it was always great to finally meet people in person.

WHAT'S THE PROJECT STATUS?

NICE TO *FINALLY* MEET YOU!

LIKEWISE!

Due to a company reorganization we had merged some departments, so this particular trip would also be an opportunity to meet several new team members too.

A few of us were able to fly in the day before. So we decided to have a group dinner at San Francisco's famous Pier 39.

PIER 39

Given that we had all started to work together virtually a few months before, we were already familiar with some of our newer teammates.

It was a fun dinner with these people, some of whom would become friends for years to come.

Since we had taken a taxi to Pier 39, we needed to take a taxi to get back to the hotel. However, there was an unusually long line of people waiting for a ride. I and Laura, a new coworker, decided to forego waiting.

'NIGHT!

SEE YOU TOMORROW!

It was a nice night so she and I decided to hang out at the tourist trap for a bit, thinking it better to spend the time browsing in the nearby shops.

I DON'T HAVE A PREFERENCE.

THEN LET'S GO INTO THAT ONE!

GIFT SHOP

Now, one of the major tourist appeals about Pier 39 is that it offers a great view of the infamous prison island Alcatraz from the end of the pier.

Because of this close proximity, a few gift shops offered a wide variety of completely cheesy Alcatraz-related souvenirs.

As Laura and I made snarky comments about the tacky souvenirs, we came across a clearance section.

CLEARANCE

Laura and I clearly shared a subversive sense of humor as we eyed boxes of novelty handcuffs and dared each other to buy one (for no particular reason.)

In one of the few times I took a dare, I bought one but she didn't. (I can't remember her excuse.)

I don't know if Laura knew then that I am a lesbian, but if she did, it would have been via the rumor mill, which was fine with me.*

We had fun with that little distraction and, sure enough, the taxi line was down after it was over.

* IN READING THIS STORY, LAURA ADMITTED SHE DIDN'T KNOW I WAS A LESBIAN THEN. SHE JUST LIKED MY SENSE OF HUMOR.

Once I got back to the hotel, I put the cuffs into my carry-on bag and turned in for the night, knowing that the next two days would be busy with back-to-back group meetings. I hadn't even taken the cuffs out of the box since it was joke purchase.

The next two days were filled with meetings that were informative and productive but draining.

Some people may think business trips are just excuses to party but my company wasn't like that.

The second and final day of the meeting ended early enough that those of us who had flights could leave for the airport.

Since this was before 9/11, the security process was having your I.D. checked, carry-on bags screened, and walking through metal detectors. There could still be lines at times.

I was a seasoned corporate traveler, and security checkpoints were a breeze for me.

So I was naturally a little confused when the checkpoint guard told me to wait a minute.

Since this was "rush hour" at the airport with hundreds of business people trying to get on their flights, I admit I felt a little self-conscious for holding up the line.

I then noticed that my coworkers who had passed through were standing and waiting, looking just as baffle as I was.

SORRY!

WHAT'S GOING ON?

Of course, this had to be the one time ultra-conservative, religious zealot Rose The Office Admin* tried to joke with me.

INTERNALLY ROLLING MY EYES.

WERE YOU BUSTED FOR DRUGS?

DON'T KNOW.

*SEE THE STORY "THE REPUBLICAN TOASTMASTER"

Remember, this was before 9/11.

Because I had arrived earlier than my local teammates, I was on a separate flight back to Irvine.

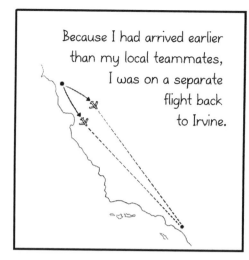

That was fine with me since it meant I could avoid the expected teasing about the handcuffs that everyone now knew I had.

The next day at work, I found out that my coworkers on the other flight had a gleeful time of their own.

YEAH, TELL HER!

IT WAS HILARIOUS!

YOU SHOULDA BEEN THERE!

REALLY?

Predictably, *EVERYONE* knew about my handcuffs before the flights. They told me that they used them as an excuse to talk about bondage just to piss off Rose, whose ultra-conservative ways did not make her popular in the office. (I swear: I did *not* tell them to do that! Yes, I'm aware this is a definition of "hostile work environment." But then, Rose is no less guilty.)

Yes, it was evil and definitely didn't help Rose make friends with the rest of us. I'm more surprised that no one called Human Resources on each other.

Still, it was a great lunch story to bring out every once in a while.

As for my Bellevue coworker Laura, when she was found out about what happened to me at airport security, she was stuck in rush hour traffic and could not stop laughing.

She admitted she very glad that she didn't buy a pair herself.

And every time I tell this story, people ask me where the handcuffs are now. I tell them the truth: I totally forgot — just like when I put them in the suitcase the first time.

My own lesson from this whole incident: It's one thing to have your coworkers know you're a lesbian activist. It's quite another to have them think you're into bondage.

Luckily, no one has ever asked me about the latter because my answer would be disappointing.

– END –

86

In Spring 1990, I became a Co-Chair of the Gay And Lesbian Student Union at UCI. Having been a member since early '88, I was now one of the two people in charge of the GLSU as well as representing it to the university administration.

GLSU

The timing was significant, not just for me but for UCI and Orange County as well.

In Sept. '89, Orange County held its first gay and lesbian pride festival at another city in Orange County to infamous results.

Got AIDS Yet?

Homo sex is a sin

To avoid a repeat of hostilities, the decision was made to hold the 1990 festival at UCI.

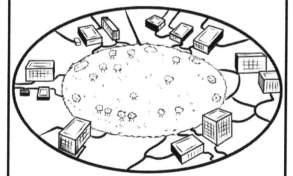

The campus was designed in a large circle with a nice park in the middle with lush grass and lots of trees.

As part of the '90 festival, The NAMES Project brought the AIDS Memorial Quilt as its OC debut.

As a Co-Chair of the GLSU, I was asked to be one of the readers at the opening dedication ceremony, which is a great honor.

If you have not heard of the AIDS Memorial Quilt, each panel represents someone who passed from AIDS.

Each panel is the size of a coffin, and each helps people process their grief while memorializing their lost loved one.

Each added panel visually shows the growing impact of the disease, not only in numbers but also in the diversity of individuals lost.

At various cities across the U.S., panels would be added in dedication ceremonies.

And while many considered the AIDS Crisis officially over, people are still passing from the disease and the AIDS Memorial Quilt continues to grow to this day.

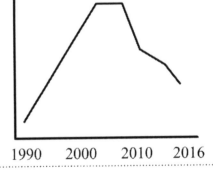

TO MAKE A QUILT, DONATE OR SEE A VIEWING, GO TO WWW.AIDSQUILT.ORG.

When I came out of the closet in 1987, at the age of 19, I did it "cold" in that I didn't really know anyone else who was queer. No family members, no friends, not even acquaintances.

Obviously, if they were queer but not out, I and everyone else were none the wiser.

To solve this isolation, I volunteered for queer organizations.

While it developed my social circles, I also liked helping out in the ways a starving college student could.

At the time of that first AIDS Memorial Quilt viewing, I hadn't personally lost anyone to AIDS. I didn't even know anyone who was diagnosed or sick.

While I had heard about it, I had never seen the AIDS Memorial Quilt in person prior to my participation in that OC dedication ceremony.

EACH LIST CORRESPONDS TO A SET OF PANELS.

But I was fully committed to giving this experience my most serious and earnest participation.

WHEN YOU FINISH YOUR LIST, WE ENCOURAGE YOU TO ADD THE NAMES OF PEOPLE YOU KNEW WHO PASSED FROM AIDS, WHETHER OR NOT THEY HAVE A PANEL.

JACK JONES, BOBBY SMITH, ALEX...

Even though I had been to my fair share of public speaking events, this one was extremely different in terms of the intense somberness and sorrow.

When it was my turn, it took every ounce of self-control for me to keep my voice from cracking or a tear welling up in my eye.

My only regret of that moment is that I did not have a personal name to add to the list.

After my reading, I walked around the displayed panels, knowing that they were only a fraction of the entire Quilt, even then.

As far as panel recognition, the only names I recognized were celebrities like Rock Hudson and Waylon Flowers.*

* Seeing his panel shocked me as I was a huge fan of Madame as a kid and had no clue of the gay sensibilities of the act.

I remember noticing the boxes of tissues that were ready on the floor.

If people talked, it was in whispers.

The loudest noises were from a few people who were fully sobbing.

The profoundness of the experience stayed with me for several years.

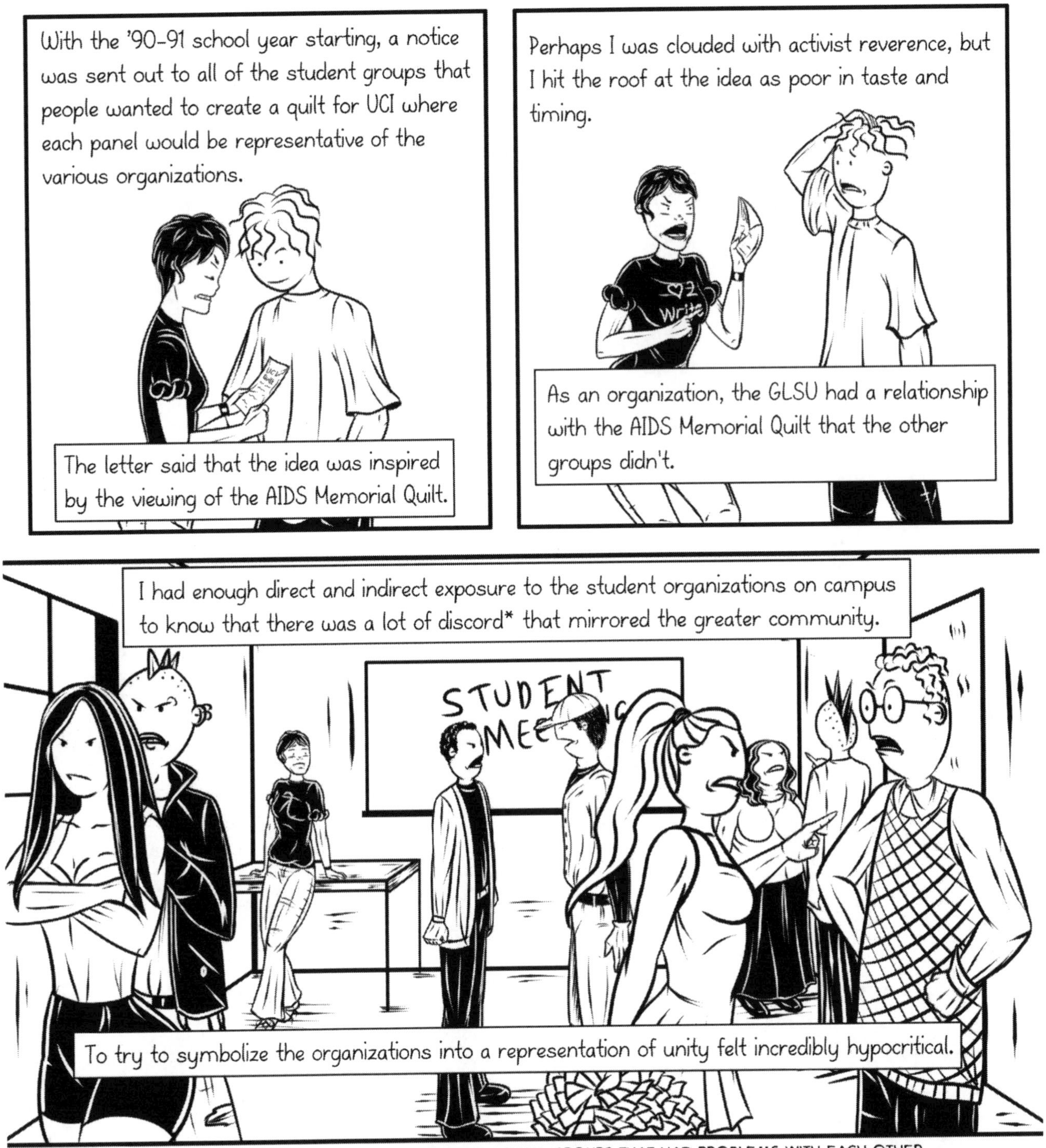
With the '90-91 school year starting, a notice was sent out to all of the student groups that people wanted to create a quilt for UCI where each panel would be representative of the various organizations.
The letter said that the idea was inspired by the viewing of the AIDS Memorial Quilt.
Perhaps I was clouded with activist reverence, but I hit the roof at the idea as poor in taste and timing.
As an organization, the GLSU had a relationship with the AIDS Memorial Quilt that the other groups didn't.
I had enough direct and indirect exposure to the student organizations on campus to know that there was a lot of discord* that mirrored the greater community.
STUDENT
To try to symbolize the organizations into a representation of unity felt incredibly hypocritical.

* DISCLAIMER: NO, THE ABOVE PANEL DO NOT SHOW THE ACTUAL GROUPS THAT HAD PROBLEMS WITH EACH OTHER.

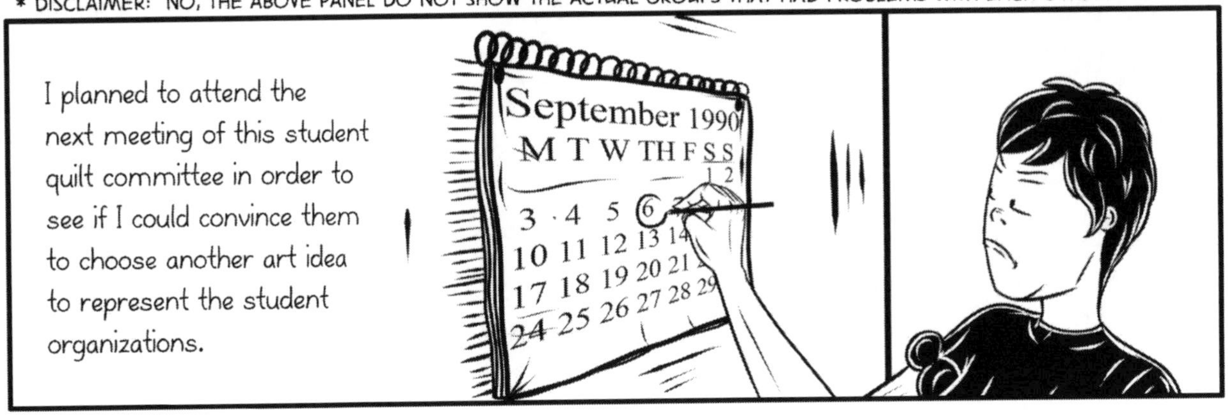
I planned to attend the next meeting of this student quilt committee in order to see if I could convince them to choose another art idea to represent the student organizations.
September 1990
M T W TH F S S

At that meeting I made my most impassioned plea that this UCI Quilt proposal was a bad idea by explaining what the AIDS Memorial Quilt was really about and citing AIDS Quilt statistics.

Then the committee members rightfully pointed out that the quilt concept was an American tradition that shouldn't be monopolized as a symbol by a single group.

Their minds were clearly set on the idea.

I didn't succeed in changing their plans but I was glad I had made my views known.

My distaste of the idea led me to wash my hands of it so my partner co-chair took over the project from the GLSU perspective.

I admit it caused an interesting discussion within our group: What should a quilt panel look like to represent a queer student organization for years and perhaps decades to come?

Even though I didn't succeed in my quest to convince the quilt committee to choose another idea, I started to get private feedback from some committee members that they too weren't keen on the idea for the very reasons I had brought up.

Then the leader of a student organization approached the quilt committee with a list of OTHER student organizations that they did NOT want to be their "panel neighbors."

I never saw the list but I would bet a million bucks that the GLSU was on it.

Admittedly, the cynical part of me couldn't imagine the GLSU being a group others would WANT our panel to be next to theirs.

I told the others in the GLSU about the existence of the No-Neighbor list and their reactions mirrored mine.

The committee members then proposed the idea of each organization having an independent display case that could be hosted around the various public areas of the student center, an idea I fully supported.

That incident opened my eyes to the different ways people can show homophobia and exclusion.

A message that was the complete opposite of its inspiration, the AIDS Memorial Quilt.

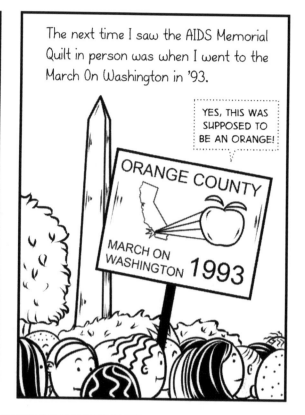

The next time I saw the AIDS Memorial Quilt in person was when I went to the March On Washington in '93.

YES, THIS WAS SUPPOSED TO BE AN ORANGE!

ORANGE COUNTY

MARCH ON WASHINGTON 1993

Even though the event was only three years later, by then I was more aware of friends and acquaintances who had passed on from the disease or were Living as a Person With AIDS.

It's not a then vs. now comparison that makes me feel better.

For me, it became yet another experience as a lesbian activist that should be valued and cherished. And hopefully it won't repeat itself in my lifetime or anyone else's.

– END –

Poster Patrol

Story: P. Kristen Enos ~ Art: Casandra Grullon

In the late '80's, the UCI Gay & Lesbian Student Union had limited options for promoting our events on campus.

Like all organizations at the time, we maintained a mailing list that consisted of names, postal mailing address and/or phone numbers, from people filling out sign-up sheets, usually with crappy handwriting.

Even though we declared confidentiality, it was hardly a list that could be treated with full confidence in its accuracy.

Some people would put just first names or fake names which caused confusion when you met them at GLSU events.

When we sent out mailings, for the return address, we would put the organization initials or no name at all.

Before the days of private cell phones, phones were usually shared lines with roommates, who usually didn't know about someone's queer nature. So calling people needed to be done carefully.

Once, I was staffing the office when I received a call from a male student who asked to be put on the mailing list. I took the call seriously until I heard female giggles in the background.

SURE, I'LL PUT YOUR NAME ON OUR LIST.

I pretended to write down "his" info and hung up.

Sure enough, the next day, I received a panicked call from the guy identifying himself as the real person and wanting to confirm that I hadn't put him on our list.

IT'S **OKAY!**

I **DIDN'T** PUT YOU ON OUR MAILING LIST!

YOU SURE?! CUZ I'M **NOT** GAY!

His fear caused by the attempted practical joke was very real.

One way to advertise our events was through the UCI gay & lesbian newspaper.

HERE'S THE GLSU SCHEDULE FOR THE QUARTER.

OKAY, I'LL ASSIGN SOMEONE TO INTERVIEW YOU.

But it also had a limited budget and could only publish quarterly, which meant a lot of planning in advance.

It was an effective tool to get the word out to people who wanted to remain as anonymous as possible. Providing the copies weren't thrown out by disapproving folks.

GAY & Lesbian

But the most effective, last minute publicity — a method shared by all campus student groups — was to post flyers or banners in key public places.

However, it was common occurrence for our particular group to have our ads ripped down almost as soon as they were put up.

Ironically, I can't remember anyone ever defacing our posters with rude comments or pictures.

It was like the sight of the banner was offensive enough to be gotten rid of as soon as possible.

It wasn't worth complaining to campus administration about the removal of our banners.

We expected it to happen and it always did.

Because of these experiences, the GLSU developed what we called "Poster Patrol"

The process was simple: When we had an upcoming event like a dance, we would get as many people together as possible to create promotional signs of paper with paint or markers.

We made big banners because people could read these from a distance.

We would then ration out the banners to be posted.

Then we would assign people to make the campus rounds to replace torn down posters.

The people posting the banners had to be out since they could be seen doing such a controversial activity.

And it was even better to do it in pairs or more just as a means of hanging out and having fun.

Since I preferred activities to make or strengthen friendships, this one time I volunteered with Nico.

WANT TO DO IT TOGETHER?

SURE!

MULTI-CULTURAL AMERICANS

SAME TASTE IN MUSIC

We spent our poster patrol time checking for banners and replacing them as needed while chitchatting about random topics.

GEEKS

STILL FRIENDS TO THIS DAY, 30 YEARS LATER

And, of course, being public as queer activists on campus wasn't an issue for us. Or so we thought.

NICO!

KRISTEN!

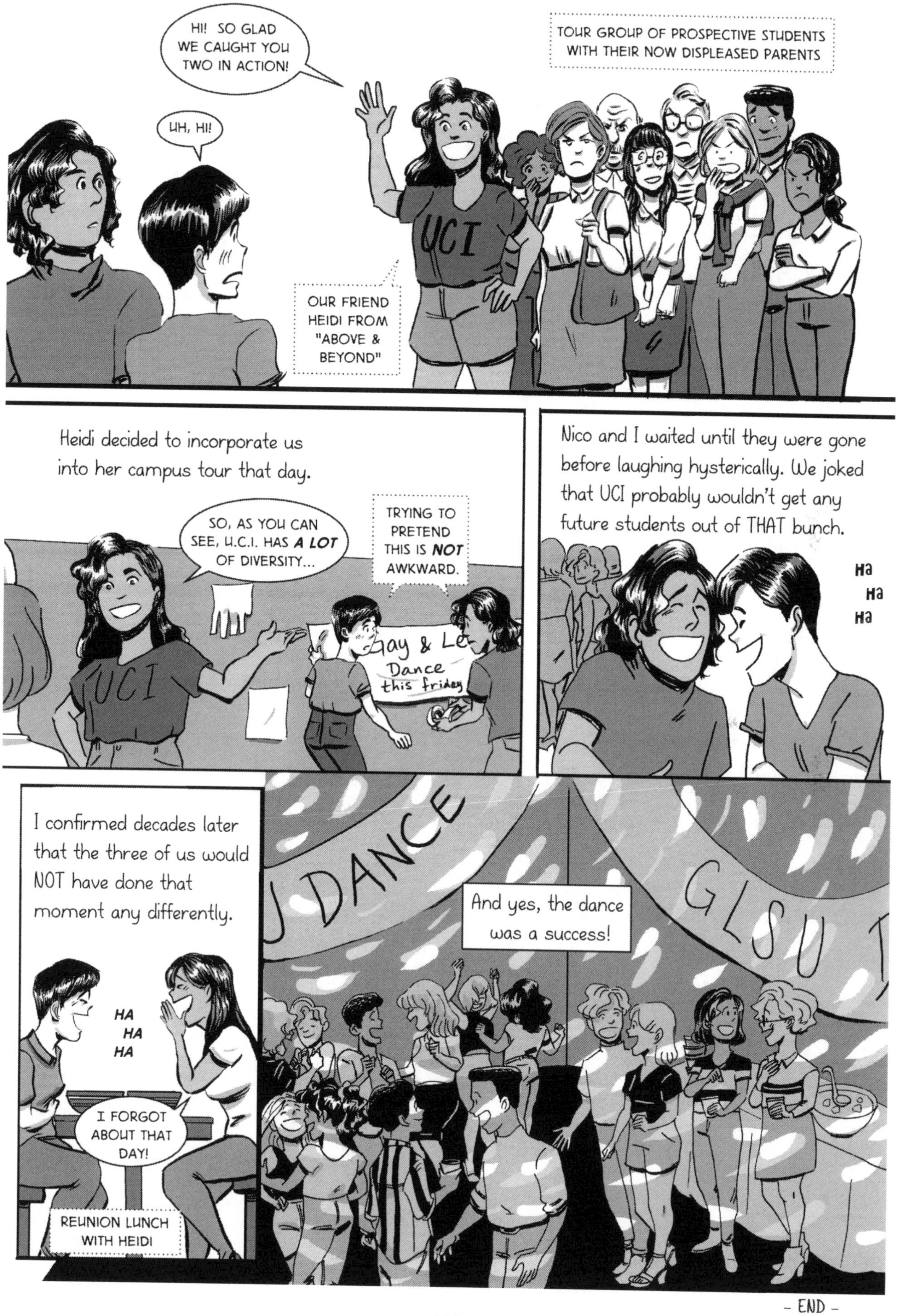
HI! SO GLAD WE CAUGHT YOU TWO IN ACTION!
TOUR GROUP OF PROSPECTIVE STUDENTS WITH THEIR NOW DISPLEASED PARENTS
UH, HI!
OUR FRIEND HEIDI FROM "ABOVE & BEYOND"
Heidi decided to incorporate us into her campus tour that day.
SO, AS YOU CAN SEE, U.C.I. HAS A LOT OF DIVERSITY...
TRYING TO PRETEND THIS IS NOT AWKWARD.
Dance this friday
Nico and I waited until they were gone before laughing hysterically. We joked that UCI probably wouldn't get any future students out of THAT bunch.
Ha Ha Ha
I confirmed decades later that the three of us would NOT have done that moment any differently.
HA HA HA
I FORGOT ABOUT THAT DAY!
REUNION LUNCH WITH HEIDI
DANCE
GLSU
And yes, the dance was a success!

- END -

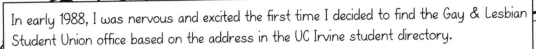

In early 1988, I was nervous and excited the first time I decided to find the Gay & Lesbian Student Union office based on the address in the UC Irvine student directory.

I admit I was completely nervous as I didn't know what to expect or how I would act if I encountered someone there.

It turned out that the office was located in the tiny Humanities Trailer park, which was off the main walkway. The five or six office trailers were packed together in a small grove of trees, a sharp contrast to the polished and futuristic design of the rest of the campus buildings.

When I saw that the office was closed, I felt mixture of relief (in my baby-steps of coming out publically) and annoyance (in wanting to socially connect as soon as possible.)

Gay & Lesbian Student Center

CLOSED

I would try stopping by again on random days and times of day. Each time it would be closed.

I FINALLY came when a guy had just left the office.

After welcoming me, he then told me about the weekly meetings the GLSU held at the Women's Resource Center.

HI!

CLOSED

IT'S EVERY WEDNESDAY NIGHT.

I'LL BE THERE!

So I attended my first GLSU meeting, which happened to be an AIDS Awareness Workshop.

I was glad that while it was mostly guys, there were a couple of women there too.

It was my night for a lot of firsts.

I quickly became friends with many of the GLSU members.

And they quickly became used to the idea that I usually had a camera on me.*

Having had one since I was a child, I viewed the camera as both a tool and a toy to capture interactions between people. And my new GLSU friends were always willing to accommodate.

A year later, I was surprised when Nico, one of the Co-Chairs of the GLSU, asked to borrow my camera for a moment.

I JUST NEED IT FOR AN HOUR.

SURE!

The seriousness and urgency of his tone was very evident.

* THIS WAS LONG BEFORE DIGITAL CAMERAS AND SPONTANEOUS SELFIES.

Someone had thrown a rock through the window of the GLSU trailer office and Nico needed to document the vandalism.

It was the first time something like that had happened and we members were understandably shocked.

Thankfully, the university administration recognized and treated it as the act of violence that it was. They even sent a counselor to speak at one of the student union meetings.

The window was fixed quickly, and people wouldn't have known about the incident if they hadn't been told.

It made me glad for once that the office was located well out of sight of most student traffic.

Still, someone just coming out could have seen the office in its vandalized state.

I think it would have been enough to scare them back several steps into the closet, if not permanently.

For me, I felt that the timing worked in my favor since I had already been involved with the GLSU for a year at the time. The incident was just another aspect of my budding lesbian activist life.

CHANGING OVER OFFICE HOUR SHIFTS

SEE YA!

BYE!

As for the person* who actually threw the rock, I have no doubt it was an important event for them for all of the wrong, and sadly pitiful reasons.

The incident was so minor in my personal history that I'm only reminded of it when I browse through my photo albums, where I kept Nico's photos for historical reference.

WHAT IS – OH!

* YES, IT COULD HAVE BEEN A WOMAN OR MORE THAN ONE INDIVIDUAL

When I decided to do this comic collection, I realized I needed to go back to UCI and take reference photos for my artists for some of my stories.

SHOOT, I DON'T HAVE A PICTURE OF THAT!

In the now 30 years since I first arrived, the campus has gone through significant changes and growth, in both student population and buildings.

One of the key changes was that the Humanities Trailer Park, the former home of the GLSU office, was torned down long ago and replaced by a fancy building complex. The GLSU office was moved to the redesigned student center.

DO I **NEED** ONE?

CAN WE FAKE IT?

In 1994, after I left UCI, the LGBT Resource Center opened on campus. This provided a more formal and broader queer presence on campus that the GLSU couldn't always provide.

UGH, THAT MEANS I'D HAVE TO DRIVE TO CALIFORNIA!*

And not only that, several more queer-related student organizations have since established themselves on the campus.

Still, despite all of those social changes (and hassles), I felt it wouldn't hurt to make a photo trip to the campus just in case something would help my artists.

* APPROXIMATELY 270 MILES FROM LAS VEGAS

As part of my trip to take reference photos, I decided it wouldn't hurt to swing by the LGBT resource center just to see how it currently looked.

I knew it was located in the Student Center and walked over with my camera out and ready.

Welcome to
UCIrvine
Global village

Welcom
UCIrvine
Global villag

However, I didn't know EXACTLY where and decided I needed to whip out my cell phone to look up the office address via searching the campus website.

It was then that I suddenly had the "feeling" to look up.

So I did and saw something COMPLETELY unexpected.

There, on a set of windows, was a message for people like me.

I admit I was startled.

With a missing letter, it seemed that the message had been there a while.

And I was pleased that such a message was visible in the highest traffic lane for students on campus.

So of course,
I took a picture ...

... to add it to my photo collection
as another LGBT milestone
in my personal activist history.

It felt like closure of a sour memory from my GLSU days as well as a sign that progress has been made overall.

- END -

At the time of this incident, it was 1985 and I was in 11th grade, a junior in high school, in Omaha, Nebraska. My family moved there when I started 9th grade.

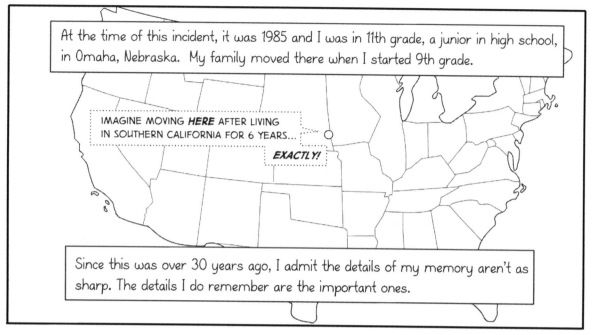

IMAGINE MOVING **HERE** AFTER LIVING IN SOUTHERN CALIFORNIA FOR 6 YEARS...

EXACTLY!

Since this was over 30 years ago, I admit the details of my memory aren't as sharp. The details I do remember are the important ones.

My English teacher gave us an assignment to form into small groups and write a story together.

My best friends at the time were in this class so we formed our own group.

Being so long ago, I don't even remember if there were two or three other girls. We were 16 years old and didn't stand out in the crowd, for the most part.

A TOMBOY (OF COURSE)

We shared a sense of playful mischief, which was very tame by 2016 standards.

Because I had created fictional stories in my brain since I was a small child, I reacted to this project with zest.

However our collective brains came up with a story that was... *unexpected.*

"Sir Limpwrist The Pink Knight"
(The original story was written in prose.)

Long ago and far away there was a man named Sir Limpwrist The Pink Knight.

He approached a powerful king to go on a quest to rescue his kidnapped princess.

The princess, the only heir to the throne, had been taken years ago and hadn't been seen or heard of since.

She was being held prisoner in a tower far, far away.

Many, many knights tried to rescue her and were killed.

I can't remember if her captor was a wizard or a witch or a dragon.

But I do remember that Sir Limpwrist was **fabulously** triumphant!

Sir Limpwrist would finally see the princess who had been hidden away for many years.

And now she was older and... bigger.

She had become so large that she couldn't walk out of her prison without risk of serious injury.

Note: The princess' weight gain makes me think that her captor was a dragon because it wanted to fatten her up for a feast.

Not one to be defeated by a challenge, Sir Limpwrist came up with a solution!

He put her on a well-rounded exercise regimen

Changed her diet

And of course, fixed her wardrobe.

Soon enough, the princess was better than ever!

The king was overjoyed to be reunited with his long-lost daughter.

As a reward, the king offered the princess' hand in marriage and therefore the crown to his kingdom.

But Sir Limpwrist had no interest and gracefully declined.

The story ended with Sir Limpwrist and the princess (now the queen) living their separate lives.

The teacher gave us an "A" for the assignment, which shocked us.

THE TEACHER DID MAKE A COMMENT ABOUT HOW THE STORY WAS PROBABLY FOR MORE "ADULT" AUDIENCES.

Now, I admit I don't remember how we came up with the story. I thought we were all heterosexual at the time. And we haven't kept in touch.

YES, I'M PROBABLY THE MOST LIKELY CULPRIT*

But we were **proud** of our achievement. No pun intended.

* I WAS A FAN OF THE MOVIE "ZORRO THE GAY BLADE" (BIG SURPRISE) EVEN IF I DIDN'T FULLY UNDERSTAND IT.

And yes, if our teacher hadn't been supportive, I'm pretty sure it still would have been a prominent childhood memory for different reasons.

In the 30 years since that incident, I've never created another character like Sir Limpwrist. And I even wrote a fantasy book in 2014 about LGBTQ pirates, *The Queens And Kings Of The Seas.*

I'm sure that aversion was the original activist in me trying to be sensitive to positive queer imagery. For the longest time a flamboyant man (who wasn't in a dress) didn't qualify.

But maybe the tide has changed now?

HMMM...

– END –

Contributors Biographies

P. KRISTEN ENOS

YES, THIS IS THE MODEL PHOTO FOR THE COVER

Given that the entire book is a collection of excerpts of my life, I almost didn't do a bio but I realized I should probably write one to fill in some missing pieces:

Kristen was born in Bangkok, Thailand but came to the US at age two and pretty much has been here since. Raised a military brat but considers herself a Southern Californian girl at heart. Went to UCI and was a double-major in Psychology and Sociology. However, she chose a well-paying corporate life over getting her degrees. And in the meantime, did all sorts of activist and creative projects on the side.

In terms of activism, Kristen has worked as a freelance journalist and event photographer for various Orange County organizations and community publications, primarily the Orange County And Long Beach Blade Newsmagazine. She has volunteered with several LGBT-related organizations, starting with the Gay & Lesbian Student Union at UCI before moving on to various non-profits in greater Orange County.

The "Active Voice" column debuted in the Orange County And Long Beach Blade Magazine in 1994 and ran for 4 years in its first run before returning to the revamped Blade California Magazine in 2012 before the magazine went on hiatus. Kristen also wrote a few original "Active Voice" columns on her personal website.

Kristen also writes and publishes the women and queer-centric, drama comic series "Web Of Lives" and its gay men-centric spinoff "Web Of Lives: Demons." A variety of comic artists support both series.

Kristen has self-published two fantasy novels "Creatures Of Grace" (Pacific Book Awards — Fantasy Finalist 2014) and "The Queens And Kings Of The Seas" (Pacific Book Awards — Fantasy Finalist 2015.)

She moved to Las Vegas in 2011 and still resides there as of this moment. But California keeps beckoning her back, a siren-song she has so far currently resisted.

For the latest information about her various projects, please check her website www.pkristenenos.com and follow her on Twitter @pkristenenos.

Contributors Biographies

HEIDI HO

Heidi Ho is an assistant professor and the Assistant Director of the Academic Support Program at University of San Francisco. She previously served as the Asian Battered Women's project attorney and managing attorney of the Asian Outreach Unit at Great Boston Legal Services. As a student at the University of San Francisco School of Law, she participated in the Academic Support Program and was the Public Interest Scholar. She has been admitted in the Bar in California, Massachusetts, and Hawaii. She graduated from UC Irvine having majored in social ecology: criminology, law, and legal studies and minored in women's studies.

JOSEPH AMSTER

Joseph Amster is a tour guide, journalist, historian, and resident of San Francisco. As a journalist, he served as editor of the LGBT publications the Orange County and Long Beach Blade and IN Los Angeles magazines. He has also had stories published in the Alyson Publications books My First Time, Vol. 1 and The Day We Met. He has served on the boards of directors of many LGBT and AIDS-related organizations.

With the rise of the Internet, Joseph found journalism jobs few and far between. In 2011 he and his husband Rick Shelton founded Time Machine Tours. Because of their backgrounds in the performing arts, they decided to offer historical walking tours as characters from San Francisco's history. Emperor Norton's Fantastic San Francisco Time Machine launched in July, 2011 to rave reviews. In 2012 Joseph combined his love of history with his culinary background to offer San Francisco Food Safari, a shopping tour of North Beach and a Mission District tour titled There's More to the Mission than Burritos in 2013. He is currently working on a book titled Created in California: The Golden State's Gifts to Gastronomy and can often be spotted about town in character as San Francisco's beloved Emperor Norton.

Contributors Biographies

DEREK CHUA

"I love to draw. If I cannot draw, I will die.
    I don't want to die, so I draw."

Derek Chua is a comic artist based in Singapore. Besides working on commissions and collaborating with other comic creators around the world, he self-publishes his own comics through his imprint, Irrational Comics.

engcheedraws.carbonmade.com
irrationalcomics.wordpress.com

LEESAMARIE CROAL

I'm an illustrator from Scotland, working in both traditional and digital mediums. I studied Visual Communication, but I am self taught with regards to my digital artwork. Currently I work as a freelance illustrator, as a penciller and colorist. I have a creator-owned comic called "The Spirit Chaser" due out on Comixology.

Facebook: Leesamarie Croal Art

Contributors Biographies

CASANDRA GRULLON

Casandra Grullon is a cartoonist and illustrator based in New York City. She graduated from the School of Visual Arts in New York City with a BFA in Cartooning. Her comics fall in various genres including romance, fantasy and horror.

Her work can be found on Behance: portfolios.sva.edu/CasandraGrullon.

BETH VARNI

A freelance illustrator of 6 years, Beth has worked in indie video games, book covers, comics, and mural painting. A graduate from VCU Arts in Richmond, VA; Beth is a big lover of video games and comics with a focus on sequential images. She has worked on many indie comics- Marked, Joshua Black, Home, Aztecman, The Witch, Poseidon, Rough Ice, and many more!

Her art can be seen at www.bethvarni.com!

Other Publications By P. Kristen Enos

Comic Book Series

Web of lives

WOMEN & QUEER-CENTRIC DRAMA
AND SUSPENSE SERIES, INCLUDING
THE WEB SERIES "BERSEKER."

Web of lives: Demons

"WEB" SPIN-OFF FEATURING DANGEROUS
GAY MEN

Zines

"ACTIVE VOICE THE ZINE" SERIES FEATURES
REPRINTS OF OLD COLUMNS WITH NEW
COMMENTARY, NEW COLUMNS (STARTING
IN ISSUE #2), STORIES BEHIND MEMORABLE
PHOTOS, AND MORE!

"THIS LESBIAN'S GUIDE TO ANIME & MANGA"
CONTAINS NEW REVIEWS ON WORKS THAT
DESERVE ANALYSIS. I ALSO HAVE A "QUICK
COMMENTS" WHERE I MAKE OBSERVATIONS
ABOUT NEWS OR WORKS THAT I WILL NOT
DO A FULL REVIEW ON.

Other Publications By P. Kristen Enos

Fantasy Fiction

Creatures Of Grace

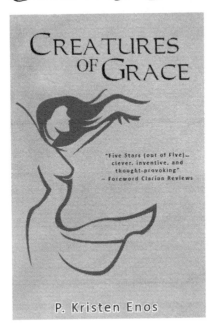

Pacific Book Awards - Fantasy Finalist 2014

A COLLECTION OF SHORT STORIES FEATURING A DIVERSE CAST OF WOMEN FACING SITUATIONS AND ISSUES OF IMPORTANCE TO THEM: A PRINCESS, A WITCH, A HOLY KNIGHT, A LESBIAN PIRATE CAPTAIN AND MORE!

The Queens And Kings Of The Seas

Pacific Book Awards - Fantasy Finalist 2015

FEATURING THE LESBIAN PIRATE CAPTAIN FROM "CREATURES OF GRACE," THIS BOOK TELLS THE STORY OF HOW HER CREW CAME TOGETHER AS PEOPLE FROM ACROSS THE QUEER SPECTRUM.

Made in the USA
Middletown, DE
11 November 2017